# A FalconGuide® to
# Dinosaur National Monument

## Help Us Keep This Guide Up to Date

Every effort has been made by the authors and editors to make this guide as accurate and useful as possible. However, many things can change after a guide is published—trails are rerouted, regulations change, techniques evolve, facilities come under new management, etc.

We would love to hear from you concerning your experiences with this guide and how you feel it could be improved and kept up to date. While we may not be able to respond to all comments and suggestions, we'll take them to heart and we'll also make certain to share them with the author. Please send your comments and suggestions to the following address:

The Globe Pequot Press
Reader Response/Editorial Department
P.O. Box 480
Guilford, CT 06437

Or you may e-mail us at:
editorial@GlobePequot.com

Thanks for your input, and happy travels!

A FALCON GUIDE®

*Exploring Series*

# A FalconGuide® to Dinosaur National Monument

## A Guide to Exploring the Great Outdoors

### Second Edition

Bert and Jane Gildart

FALCON GUIDE®

GUILFORD, CONNECTICUT
HELENA, MONTANA
AN IMPRINT OF THE GLOBE PEQUOT PRESS

**A FALCON GUIDE** ®

Maps by Trapper Badovinac with contributions by Zachary Parks © The Globe Pequot Press
All interior photos by the authors
Chapter opener photo: Views of the Green River and cliffs from Harpers Corner Trail
Graph on p. 3 courtesy of Dinosaur National Monument and the Intermountain Natural History Association

ISSN 1553-1597
ISBN 0-7627-3649-6

Manufactured in the United States of America
Second Edition/First Printing

*To our families, especially Kyle, Cassidy, Griffin, Halle, Kory, and John,
who have many years yet to explore deserts, mountains, and rivers.*

*We are now ready to start on our way down the Great Unknown.*
—John Wesley Powell, 1869


*All about me are interesting geological records.*
*The book is open, and I can read as I run.*
—John Wesley Powell, 1869

# Contents

Acknowledgments. . . . . . . . . . . . . . . . . . . . . . . . . . . . . . . xi

Map Legend. . . . . . . . . . . . . . . . . . . . . . . . . . . . . . . . . . xii

Overview Map . . . . . . . . . . . . . . . . . . . . . . . . . . . . . . . . xiii

**Chapter 1  Overview of Dinosaur National Monument** . . . . . . . 1

Creation. . . . . . . . . . . . . . . . . . . . . . . . . . . . . . . . . . . . . 1

Natural History and Other Superlatives . . . . . . . . . . . . . . . . 2

**Chapter 2  Introduction: Where to Go and What to Do** . . . . . . 5

Location . . . . . . . . . . . . . . . . . . . . . . . . . . . . . . . . . . . . . 5

Getting There. . . . . . . . . . . . . . . . . . . . . . . . . . . . . . . . . . 5

Recreational Activities . . . . . . . . . . . . . . . . . . . . . . . . . . . 5

**Chapter 3  Tips for Hiking in the High Desert: Zero Impact** . . 7

**Chapter 4  Dinosaur National Monument** . . . . . . . . . . . . . . . . 9

"The Bones" (The Quarry): Dinosaur's Jurassic Park. . . . . . 9

Location. . . . . . . . . . . . . . . . . . . . . . . . . . . . . . . . . . 9

Features . . . . . . . . . . . . . . . . . . . . . . . . . . . . . . . . . . 9

Time Required . . . . . . . . . . . . . . . . . . . . . . . . . . . . . 9

Interpretation . . . . . . . . . . . . . . . . . . . . . . . . . . . . . 9

The Quarry . . . . . . . . . . . . . . . . . . . . . . . . . . . . . . . 9

The Stories in the Rocks: Petroglyphs and Pictographs. . . 12

McKee Spring. . . . . . . . . . . . . . . . . . . . . . . . . . . . . 14

Echo Park . . . . . . . . . . . . . . . . . . . . . . . . . . . . . . . 14

Tour of the Tilted Rocks . . . . . . . . . . . . . . . . . . . . 15

Jones Hole Trail . . . . . . . . . . . . . . . . . . . . . . . . . . . 16

Mantle Cave . . . . . . . . . . . . . . . . . . . . . . . . . . . . . 16

Other Sites . . . . . . . . . . . . . . . . . . . . . . . . . . . . . . 16

Dinosaur's Bighorn Sheep . . . . . . . . . . . . . . . . . . . . . . 16

The Rivers: The Green and the Yampa. . . . . . . . . . . . . . 19

**Chapter 5  Driving Tours**. . . . . . . . . . . . . . . . . . . . . . . . . . . 21

1. Tour of the Tilted Rocks . . . . . . . . . . . . . . . . . . . . . 21

2. Harpers Corner Scenic Drive: Journey through Time. . 25

**Chapter 6  Backcountry Driving Tours** . . . . . . . . . . . . . . . . **31**

   1. Echo Park Road and Mitten Park Hike . . . . . . . . . . . . 31

      Mitten Park Hike . . . . . . . . . . . . . . . . . . . . . . . . . . . . . 35

      Echo Park . . . . . . . . . . . . . . . . . . . . . . . . . . . . . . . . . . . 36

   2. Yampa Bench Road . . . . . . . . . . . . . . . . . . . . . . . . . . . 38

**Chapter 7  Nature Hikes** . . . . . . . . . . . . . . . . . . . . . . . . . . . **43**

   1. Sound of Silence Hiking Route . . . . . . . . . . . . . . . . . . 43

   2. Desert Voices Nature Trail . . . . . . . . . . . . . . . . . . . . . 47

   3. Cold Desert Trail . . . . . . . . . . . . . . . . . . . . . . . . . . . . . 51

   4. Plug Hat Trail . . . . . . . . . . . . . . . . . . . . . . . . . . . . . . . 54

   5. Harpers Corner Trail . . . . . . . . . . . . . . . . . . . . . . . . . . 55

   6. Gates of Lodore Nature Trail . . . . . . . . . . . . . . . . . . . 59

   7. Geology Trail . . . . . . . . . . . . . . . . . . . . . . . . . . . . . . . . 62

**Chapter 8  Hiking Trails** . . . . . . . . . . . . . . . . . . . . . . . . . . . **65**

   1. Green River Campground to Split Mountain
      Campground . . . . . . . . . . . . . . . . . . . . . . . . . . . . . . . 65

   2. & 3. Hog Canyon and Box Canyon Trails . . . . . . . . . . 67

   4. Jones Hole Trail and Jones Hole National
      Fish Hatchery . . . . . . . . . . . . . . . . . . . . . . . . . . . . . . 71

**Chapter 9  Additional Exploring Suggestions** . . . . . . . . . . . . **77**

   Hiking . . . . . . . . . . . . . . . . . . . . . . . . . . . . . . . . . . . . . . . 77

      Outlaw Trail . . . . . . . . . . . . . . . . . . . . . . . . . . . . . . . . 77

      Island Park Trail . . . . . . . . . . . . . . . . . . . . . . . . . . . . . 77

      Ruple Point Trail . . . . . . . . . . . . . . . . . . . . . . . . . . . . . 77

   Driving and Walking . . . . . . . . . . . . . . . . . . . . . . . . . . . . 79

      Island/Rainbow Park Road . . . . . . . . . . . . . . . . . . . . . 79

**Chapter 10  Exploring Dinosaur National Monument
        by River** . . . . . . . . . . . . . . . . . . . . . . . . . . . . . **81**

   Running the River on Your Own . . . . . . . . . . . . . . . . . . . 81

      Fees and Shuttle Service . . . . . . . . . . . . . . . . . . . . . . . 81

      What You Need . . . . . . . . . . . . . . . . . . . . . . . . . . . . . . 82

   Running the River with a Company . . . . . . . . . . . . . . . . 83

The Green River. . . . . . . . . . . . . . . . . . . . . . . . . . . . . . . . 85
   Overview: The Enduring Green . . . . . . . . . . . . . . . . . 87
   Running the Green. . . . . . . . . . . . . . . . . . . . . . . . . . . 88
The Yampa River . . . . . . . . . . . . . . . . . . . . . . . . . . . . . 101
   Overview: The Yampa River. . . . . . . . . . . . . . . . . . . 103
   Running the Yampa. . . . . . . . . . . . . . . . . . . . . . . . . . 104

Appendices. . . . . . . . . . . . . . . . . . . . . . . . . . . . . . . . . . . 113
  Appendix A  Where to Stay While Visiting Dinosaur
    National Monument. . . . . . . . . . . . . . . . . . . . . . . . 113
  Appendix B  Dinosaur National Monument Contacts . . . 117
  Appendix C  Commercial Raft Companies and Shuttles . 119
  Appendix D  Weather, What to Bring, and
    General Tips . . . . . . . . . . . . . . . . . . . . . . . . . . . . . 121
  Appendix E  Books and Readings of Related Interest. . . . 123
  Appendix F  Additional Contacts. . . . . . . . . . . . . . . . . . 125

About the Authors. . . . . . . . . . . . . . . . . . . . . . . . . . . . . 127

# Acknowledgments

Exploring Dinosaur National Monument was a wonderful experience, made much easier by the support and friendship of many people we met along the way.

Thanks to David Whitman, Chief of Interpretation, for his time, for information, and for providing feedback on the book; to Christy Wright, river operations, Richard Jehle, Yampa District interpreter, and members of the Intermountain Natural History Association for their input; to seasonal naturalist Michael Erickson for his wealth of geological information and for showing us special places; and to old friend Dave Pannebaker, district ranger, for reviewing the maps and text.

We are grateful also to Meg Hatch of Hatch River Expeditions for her graciousness in enabling us to take part in a Yampa River trip, thus giving us the opportunity to explore the river and learn much about rafting from her excellent guides (as well as partaking in some fantastic meals cooked along the river).

Geri Ware, owner of Bedrock RV Campground in Jensen, Utah, provided us with friendship and a "home away from home." Thanks, Geri. Todd Wilkins, our vehicle transport person, had our truck safely waiting for us at the end of our Green River trip. We're grateful to many new friends, Charlie and Sheila Fleischman, river rats Rob, Penny, Attila, and Fred, for many kindnesses. And to all those we may have inadvertently omitted, our apologies. You know who you are—we appreciate your help.

We hope you enjoy reading this exploring book as much as we enjoyed the exploring. It represents the work of two months of time well spent discovering Dinosaur National Monument by foot, car, and raft. Any mistakes contained herein are ours. Let us know if you have a favorite spot in Dinosaur that we may have missed. We welcome ideas and suggestions and may be reached through The Globe Pequot Press, P.O. Box 480, Guilford, CT 06437. Tread lightly, and keep exploring!

# Map Legend

| | | | |
|---|---|---|---|
| U.S. Highway | ⑤ ⑤⑤ ⑤⑤⑤ | Bridge | ≍ |
| State Road | ⑤ ⑤⑤ ⑤⑤⑤ | Cave | ⤚ |
| Forest Road | 41 416 4165 | City | ◉ |
| Highway | ▬▬▬▬▬ | Campground | ⛺ |
| Paved Road | ────────── | Primitive Campsite | ▲ |
| Unpaved Road | ========= | Directions | ↖ |
| Trailhead | START | Mile Marker | 🚩 24 🚩 |
| Trail(s) | - - - - - - - - - | Meadow | � |
| Route | · · · · · · · · · · · | Overlook | 👁 |
| River | ∿∿∿∿ | Parking Area | 🅿 |
| Creek | ∼∼∼ | Park Headquarters/ Visitor Center | 🏠 |
| Dry Wash | ∿∿∿∿ | Peak | ▲ |
| Rapids | ∿WWW∿ | Picnic Area | ⚎ |
| Spring | ⚲ | Point of Interest | ▢ |
| State Border | ─ · ─ · ─ COLORADO | Ranger Station | ▮ |
| Canyon Boundary | ─ ─ ─ ─ ─ | Structure | ▪ |
| Monument Boundary | ▭ ▭ ▭ ▭ | Trail Marker | ◆➋ |
| Cliffs | ⩗⩘⩗ | | |

# Dinosaur National Monument

## Creation

In 1909 on a sultry August day, a tired and somewhat frustrated man by the name of Earl Douglass began digging what he thought would be his last excavation of the summer. Douglass was digging in a geological layer known as the Morrison Formation, and he was searching for dinosaur bones and for small and prehistoric mammalian bones—his specialty. Douglass knew the area contained such remains, though it was the dinosaur bones that had eluded him throughout the summer. Despite the late hour of the day, Douglass struggled on, but he had a train to catch and a family to consider.

Suddenly Douglass noted a large prominent bone protruding from the side of the hill. Carefully he chipped away at the tomb of dirt. With his brush he cleaned the surface and then discovered that this bone was attached to seven others. Moments later he discovered that those seven vertebrae were in turn attached to yet other bones and that the whole assemblage composed an immense skeleton belonging to one of North America's largest dinosaurs. Though Douglass didn't realize it at the moment, he was on the verge of discovering the remains of an *Apatosaurus*, one of the many sauropods that roamed North America about 100 million years ago during the middle of the Jurassic period.

Before his discovery of bones that day, Douglass had been prepared to return to Chicago, where he was working for Andrew Carnegie of the famous Carnegie Institute. But after notifying the millionaire of his find, Carnegie requested Douglass to stay on.

Douglass continued his work and eventually realized that the bones from this quarry exceeded the numbers of bones taken from any other quarry in North America. So remain Douglass did. For twenty years he remained, working until he ultimately revealed that not only did the site contain extensive numbers of bones but that it also provided specimens of more than one-half of all the species of dinosaurs thought to have roamed throughout North America.

Several years after these excavations, news reached sympathetic ears, and in 1915 President Woodrow Wilson established Dinosaur National Monument by presidential proclamation. Wilson wanted the monument to protect these rich finds from commercial interests, which it did. Today, of course, Dinosaur National Monument does much more: It offers fascinating examples of geology, of flora and fauna, and of signs of early-day Native Americans. What's more, by virtue of its assorted trails and world-class white-water rivers, the monument offers incredible ways to explore these features.

## Natural History and Other Superlatives

Our country's monuments have always been associated with interesting geological phenomena, and that is certainly true in Dinosaur. Here the monument harbors one of the most complete geological records found anywhere in North America. Dinosaur's record of geological history, spanning 1.1 billion years, is ancient—nearly as old as the oldest known rocks in the Grand Canyon of the Colorado River.

If, as geologists say, the world is more than four billion years old, that means one-quarter of the world's history can be studied in Dinosaur—an area one-half the size of Rhode Island.

In a word, the rocks here are old—so old they create only an abstraction. Who can really relate to 1.1 billion years? Humans, after all, are thought to have stepped on the face of the earth rather recently—about one million years ago, say anthropologists. These rocks and their various strata are the result of the encroachment of twelve different seas and their associated periods of deposition.

All this rock assumes a multitude of different forms. The red rock tends to belong to a formation known as the Moenkopi and Carmel Formation; the gray rock, the white rock, the black rock, and all the variations in between belong to other formations.

As the eons progressed, the greatly modified rocks came to provide habitat for a number of different types of flora and fauna. First they provided habitat for a variety of species of plants. Then with time they attracted dinosaurs. Much more recently the rocks and plants began to provide for bighorn sheep, deer, and elk. They provide for a multitude of birds as well.

One of the most conspicuous of all these species is the bighorn sheep. Bighorn sheep began arriving on the scene almost 50,000 years ago, having first drifted over from Asia and then descended down the Rocky Mountain cordiollera. With all of its mountain crevasses, the monument provides exceptional escape terrain, as you will soon realize if you begin either rafting the rivers or hiking the trails.

In total, the monument houses about 68 different species of mammals, 219 species of birds, and more than 600 species of plants in 75 different families. As you can see, traveling naturalists are offered a variety of subjects that should certainly engage their interest.

Fortunately, too, there are ways to access these spectacles. The monument offers about 110 miles of paved and unpaved roads, about 21 miles of trails (16.5 miles developed), and yet more possibilities for those willing to strike out across country.

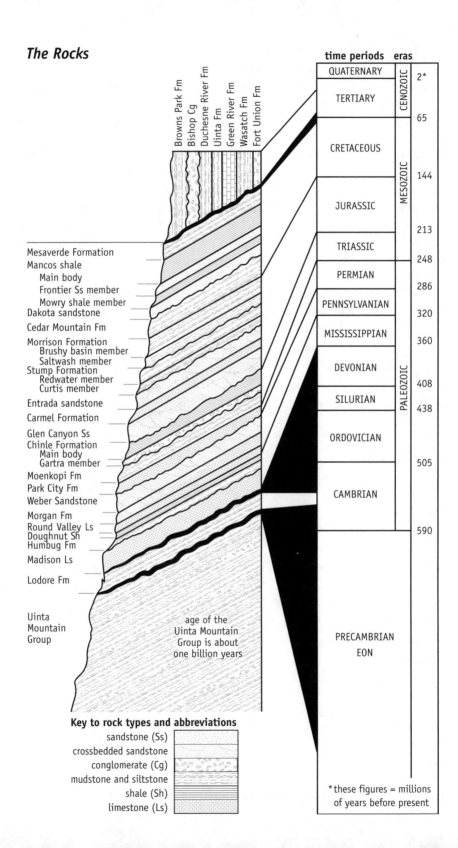

# The Rocks

time periods | eras

| | | 2* |
|---|---|---|
| QUATERNARY | CENOZOIC | |
| TERTIARY | | 65 |
| CRETACEOUS | MESOZOIC | 144 |
| JURASSIC | | 213 |
| TRIASSIC | | 248 |
| PERMIAN | | 286 |
| PENNSYLVANIAN | | 320 |
| MISSISSIPPIAN | | 360 |
| DEVONIAN | PALEOZOIC | 408 |
| SILURIAN | | 438 |
| ORDOVICIAN | | 505 |
| CAMBRIAN | | 590 |
| PRECAMBRIAN EON | | |

Browns Park Fm
Bishop Cg
Duchesne River Fm
Uinta Fm
Green River Fm
Wasatch Fm
Fort Union Fm

Mesaverde Formation
Mancos shale
  Main body
   Frontier Ss member
   Mowry shale member
Dakota sandstone
Cedar Mountain Fm
Morrison Formation
  Brushy basin member
  Saltwash member
Stump Formation
  Redwater member
  Curtis member
Entrada sandstone
Carmel Formation
Glen Canyon Ss
Chinle Formation
  Main body
  Gartra member
Moenkopi Fm
Park City Fm
Weber Sandstone
Morgan Fm
Round Valley Ls
Doughnut Sh
Humbug Fm
Madison Ls
Lodore Fm
Uinta Mountain Group

age of the Uinta Mountain Group is about one billion years

**Key to rock types and abbreviations**

| | |
|---|---|
| sandstone (Ss) | |
| crossbedded sandstone | |
| conglomerate (Cg) | |
| mudstone and siltstone | |
| shale (Sh) | |
| limestone (Ls) | |

*these figures = millions of years before present

The monument also offers two world-class white-water rivers: the Yampa and the Green. They, too, have fascinating features and histories. Though trappers and others attempted to explore them for their furs, they were not mapped and described until John Wesley Powell struck out one day in 1869. Though Powell remains best known for his explorations of what is now the Grand Canyon, he was both enchanted and alarmed by the beauty and the ferocity of the Green. If you float the Green, just below Lodore you'll pass the site where he almost lost one of his old boats. Not much farther along, you'll come to the place where the one-armed Civil War veteran almost lost his life.

Though river travel can still be dangerous, today rubber rafts and other high-tech equipment have reduced some of the horrors known to early-day floaters. Many of these techniques were pioneered by Jens Jensen and Bert Loper, men who became famous in their own right—first by running rapids, then by inaugurating some of North America's first commercial river trips.

This brings us to a discussion of how best to explore Dinosaur and, in turn, leads to a more thorough discussion of just what the monument has to offer.

# Chapter 2
# Introduction:
# Where to Go and What to Do

## Location

Dinosaur National Monument is easily located by looking at a map in either northeastern Utah or northwestern Colorado. Dinosaur straddles the two states, allocating about two-thirds of its 330 square miles to Colorado and the other one-third to Utah.

Though Dinosaur incorporates part of the Great Basin high desert, it also includes mountains characteristic of the Rockies. It ranges in elevation from about 4,700 feet along the Green River to 9,006 feet atop Zenobia Peak. With such variation in elevation, it's little wonder temperatures can vary 140 degrees Fahrenheit in a single year. Summers sometimes push the mercury higher than 100 degrees, and winter draws it down to 30 or 40 below zero.

## Getting There

Dinosaur National Monument lies at the edge of the Great Basin Desert between northeastern Utah and northwestern Colorado.

From Salt Lake City, 170 miles west of the monument, take Interstate 80 east to U.S. Highway 40/189 south to Heber City. Take US 40 east to Vernal. Continue 13 miles on US 40 east to Jensen, where signs are posted to take Utah Highway 149 north (left), 7 miles to the Monument Quarry entrance station. An entrance fee is required.

From Craig, Colorado (90 miles east of Dinosaur Headquarters Visitor Center and 42 miles west of Steamboat Springs), take US 40 west 90 miles to the large sign on the right for the park. This is the canyon land part of the monument and the Headquarters Visitor Center; no entrance fee is required. Douglass Dinosaur Quarry is 25 miles more to the west on US 40, then 7 miles north on UT 149.

Beginning your exploration from either place would be acceptable, though when time is limited, most choose to begin with a tour of Douglass Dinosaur Quarry. Spring and fall are probably the best times to visit the monument, but Dinosaur is open year-round and can be easily accessed from US 40.

## Recreational Activities

There is something for everyone in Dinosaur National Monument. Take your pick of touring the dinosaur quarry (kids love it), going on driving tours, hiking, backpacking, white-water river running, photography, bird-watching, fishing, general sightseeing, biking, and getaway relaxation. In his comprehensive book *Wild Country Companion*, Will Harmon states that in a recent study of noise levels, "Dinosaur National Monument ranks as the country's quietest place at eleven decibels (by comparison a whisper rattles the ears at fifteen to thirty decibels)." Dinosaur has another thing going for it: clean air. It can be measured by the intensity of color in the lichen on the rocks.

Though Dinosaur is not known for a large system of hiking trails, the monument contains several trails to suit just about everyone. Hiking is the best way to experience the area. More adventurous types can embark on a backcountry hike of any length. Check in with rangers for free camping permits and to obtain advice on the best areas. The biggest drawback is the large amount of water you'll need—on hot summer days, a gallon a day per person minimum!

Although there are no designated mountain biking trails in the monument, routes do exist on which you can ride. Bikes are allowed on paved and unpaved roads but not on trails or two-track backcountry roads. The roads are narrow with no shoulders. The following three areas are suggested for mountain bike use: Island Park Road (17.4 miles to road's end) is considered easy to moderate. Echo Park Road (13 miles one-way) ends at Echo Park Campground and is unpaved, steep, rough, and strenuous. Yampa Bench Road (27 miles in the monument, plus at least 20 miles back to US 40) has no campgrounds or water and is steep in places! It is a strenuous ride, and rangers say this one takes good planning.

If you are an angler, you must have a valid fishing license and know the regulations. Fly fishing is popular at Jones Hole Creek (artificial lures and flies only), and there are northern pike and catfish in the Green and Yampa Rivers.

White-water boating is one of the most popular sports in Dinosaur, either on your own or with a professional guide outfit. Boating also takes you into the world of incredible canyons and formations—a world not as easily seen from above. Because both rivers are very cold with strong currents, swimming is not recommended. Boating permits are required.

Plan to attend talks and guided walks during your stay. In summer daily talks are presented at the dinosaur quarry, and talks occur nearly every evening at the Green River Campground. Longer walks and talks are offered daily at many locations throughout the park in summer; pick up a weekly schedule at one of the visitor centers. What you quickly learn is that a few hours spent at the monument is not enough.

The arid land of the desert is a special place, and we must remember how fragile an environment we are visiting. Most "zero impact" ethics are basically commonsense rules, but sometimes we forget what inherently makes a desert. The harsh climate and lack of water and food stress the desert life forms.

You would probably never clump around carelessly in your own flower garden, which took weeks to till and plant. Likewise, the soil and the plants of the desert are extremely fragile and cannot be trampled without long-range damage. Repair cannot happen overnight—repairs take years and often may not happen at all.

Microbiotic soil, one of the most valuable and fragile of soils, is in reality a community of organisms composed of lichen, algae, bacteria, moss, and fungi. Together these organisms form microbiotic "soil," which can fix nitrogen and stabilize the soil. This soil provides the first source of nutrients on bare, sterile, sandy, desert soil and protects those plants attempting to establish a toehold against the ravages of wind and water.

Microbiotic soil can be easily destroyed by one large boot, so please avoid going into areas where you see it. Use existing trail systems or travel on hard surfaces—in rocky washes or on rocks.

Be careful where you pitch tents in the desert backcountry, and camp away from any water sites. Don't make fires; use a cookstove instead. Carry out everything, including ashes. Be careful with human waste—if you must dig a cat hole, dig 6 to 9 inches deep and cover it well. Use river water for bathing, and always purify drinking water.

If you encounter desert wildlife, especially during the day, be careful not to startle them into running. It's difficult enough for animals to keep cool and hydrated without the added problem of human confrontations.

This brings us to another topic: human dehydration, one of the biggest dangers in desert hiking. You'll need a gallon of water a day or more if you hike in warmer weather. Always carry enough water, and turn back before you run out or discover that no water sources exist.

Sunburn is another danger. Wear a broad-brimmed hat, use plenty of sunscreen, and have a long-sleeved shirt handy.

During spring and summer, storms roll in quickly in the desert, sometimes causing flash flooding. Don't camp in washes or on low ground. Get to high

*One of the many lizards that call Dinosaur National Monument home.*

ground, even if the storm doesn't seem that near, and don't wade or drive through the water.

Snakes and other crawly things live in the desert. Watch where you sit, and don't put hands or feet into or on rocky places without looking first.

Treat the places you visit as part of your home, which they are—at least temporarily. Take care of this home for your own enjoyment and for the generations to follow.

## The "Bones" (The Quarry): Dinosaur's Jurassic Park

### Location

From U.S. Highway 40 at Jensen, Utah, turn north onto Utah Highway 149 at the sign to the monument, and proceed about 7 miles to the entrance station. Douglass Dinosaur Quarry is located on the left, several hundred yards past the entrance station. In summer, park your vehicle at the lower parking lot; from there, walk up the road for 0.5 mile or proceed to the adjacent display area to await the train that will take you to the quarry.

### Features

Dinosaur National Monument features an exhibit of more than 1,500 dinosaur fossils left in situ beneath a large shelter, which remains open year-round. The visitor center contains a paleontology laboratory, exhibits, and a bookstore.

### Time Required

Most visitors will be satisfied with a visit of one to two hours, though you could easily spend a day or even more.

### Interpretation

Most likely you'll want to begin your exploration of Dinosaur National Monument at the quarry. In addition to many excellent interpretive talks offered inside, during the summer naturalists offer an interpretive walk down the 0.5-mile road that leads to the quarry. During the walk, naturalists interpret the geology of the hills that contributed to such a collection of dinosaurs. Children's programs are offered on weekends.

### The Quarry

When you first enter the quarry and look at the 1,500 displayed fossils, you can't help but ask yourself: Did paleontologists really discover the bones as they are presented, or did someone artfully place them here for effect? The answer is that paleontologists discovered the bones just where you see them today. Everything in the quarry is real. The bones are just as nature arranged them more than 150 million years ago, deposited by an ancient stream.

*Bones in Douglass Dinosaur Quarry.*

The river coursed through a lowland area and sometimes dried up. Dinosaurs gathered around shrinking pools of water in the river bed and eventually died in place, to be entombed by sand and gravel when the river flowed once again.

With more time, the river amassed large quantities of bones. Layers of mud and sand began covering the bones, eventually hardening into rock. Here they remained, waiting for the next cataclysmic event.

About sixty-five million years ago, that event began to occur. Forces beneath the earth's crust began to exert themselves, forcing the crust upward, causing it to buckle and the riverbed containing the bones to tilt upward. Now near the surface, it was inevitable that erosion would eventually expose the bones and that one day someone would find them.

The National Park Service provides a wonderful explanation of the clues that led to these many revelations and to the incredible detective work scientists conducted. Associated with the dinosaur bones were a number of other fossils that told of a much different environment. By carefully chipping away at the surrounding stone, paleontologists found teeth, a bony back plate or scute, as well as a hip bone—all from an ancient type of crocodile. Because most crocodiles live along river systems, finding these fossils provided yet further evidence that a large river once cut through the area.

This is the evidence that awaited Earl Douglass back in 1909 and that awaited all subsequent paleontologists who excavated the mound until 1990. As these scientists examined this mass of evidence, they did what all pale-ontologists do: They dug it up, finding as they excavated enough bones to supply museums throughout America with amazing skeletal structures of crea-tures that many consider to have been some of the world's most successful inhabitants.

The extent of the scientists' findings were amazing. On a single hill, they found the remains of flesh-eating dinosaurs. They found both huge and small dinosaurs. They found *Camptosaurus* and *Dryosaurus*, dinosaurs that walked and ran on their hind legs and that had both teeth and horny beaks.

Here, too, they found a species known as *Stegosaurus*, which had a double row of plates down its back, four spikes on the end of its tail, and a small beaked skull. The quarry also contained *Allosaurus* and *Ceratosaurus*, ferocious preda-tors who walked on their hind legs. They had strong claws and gaping mouths filled with recurved serrated teeth.

Insofar as dinosaurs are concerned, the quarry not only preserves bones as yet unearthed but also provides answers to many fascinating questions that began to emerge when dinosaurs were first discovered. Where, for instance, did

*Bones in Douglass Dinosaur Quarry.*

all the dinosaurs go? How could such a huge, dominant animal disappear so completely from the face of the earth? Why aren't there any survivors?

Paleontologists offer many theories regarding the demise of dinosaurs. Perhaps early mammals ate too many dinosaur eggs. Perhaps an asteroid crashed into the earth and darkened the skies for months or years with the dust of its explosion. Perhaps there was a change in the earth's climate that was so sudden dinosaurs could not adapt.

Paleontologists offer yet another theory. Some say that perhaps all dinosaurs weren't wiped from the face of the earth and that one remains, though in a much-evolved form. That group is one of our most cherished groups, the order of Aves—the birds. How is this possible?

Many ornithologists say that scales may have been the predecessors of feathers. Is there, then, a creature that provided the link between dinosaurs and Aves? Paleontologists believe *Archaeopteryx*, which existed during the Jurassic period, may be that link. Though called a bird, its body was just like that of a small meat-eating dinosaur.

Because none of the theories satisfy all resulting questions, the extinction of dinosaurs remains one of the world's great mysteries. While here, consider hiking Geology Trail, best taken with a naturalist (see Chapter 7, Nature Hikes, page 62).

## The Stories in the Rocks: Petroglyphs and Pictographs

Both petroglyphs, forms pecked with a tool, and pictographs, forms created with pigments, are plentiful in and around Dinosaur National Monument. You can see them as you drive the monument's roads. You might see them suddenly at odd times when the light is appropriate, as we did one morning at the campground in Echo Park.

Stepping out of our tent, we began peering around. By now we had acquired a sense of where to look for images. Proper lighting has much to do with the discovery of rock art, and so it was for us early that morning. Angular light was just beginning to strike a panel about a hundred feet overhead. Strangely there was no way to reach the petroglyphs short of using ropes and pitons.

And so it was perfectly logical to peer above the surface of the ground and search the walls well overhead with binoculars for drawings. What excitement we felt when a panel of sheep drawings leaped out at us. Here a Fremont hunter had paid homage to bighorn sheep.

For days he must have pecked into the rock with his stone-chipping tool, taking time to delineate not only the animal's form but also the form of another sheep inside it. The artist then drew a hunter with his bow and arrow, so perhaps the hunter wasn't celebrating fecundity at all. Perhaps the artist was instead showing others where a dependable supply of sheep could be found. Or

*Petroglyphs such as these at McKee Spring add intrigue for those exploring the monument's more remote areas.*

perhaps he was placing a mark, informing the world that this was his hunting area and that others should stay out. No one will ever know.

Though obviously no one can supply answers for all the questions inherent in rock art, during summer a park naturalist provides interpretation based on years of observation, reading, and thinking about the many probing questions visitors often ask.

In recent years, naturalist Mary Beth Bennis-Smith has provided weekend tours of the McKee Spring petroglyphs. From associated materials and other ancient finds, she knows that Native American activity dates back 12,000 years, to the time of a culture referred to as the Paleo-Indian period. This group may have lived in shallow caves and have been much dependent on hunting.

About 8,000 years ago, another group—perhaps descendants from the Paleo-Indians—developed a distinct culture revolving around hunting and gathering. Archaeologists call this the Desert period archaic culture. The Fremont culture followed them.

The Fremont culture should not be confused with the Anasazi, a group that was located farther to the south and is most known for its impressive legacy of such structures as Mesa Verde, Chaco, Canyon de Chelly, and Hovenweep. The Fremont were characterized by their more nomadic ways, for they wandered extensively throughout the area now known as Utah.

The Fremont followed the season of the bighorn sheep, elk, and deer, all of which inhabited what is now Dinosaur National Monument. But they also hunted for rabbits and grouse, and they harvested nuts and berries. They grew beans, corn, and squash as well. And when they had time, they painted the walls with pictographs or, perhaps using sharp rocks, etched the walls with petroglyphs.

The Fremont created one of the most impressive panels of rock art at McKee Spring. According to Bennis-Smith, one of the most frequently asked questions about the panel is: Why did the Fremont create the numerous pictographs and petroglyphs found in and around Dinosaur? No one knows for sure, but many possibilities exist, leaving room for much speculation.

Some of the petroglyphs in Dinosaur are aligned in such a way that the sun touches them most directly on the day of a solstice or equinox. Perhaps these drawings were used to signify the time to plant crops. In fact, as you wander along the cliff face, you'll see drawings that assume many shapes and alignments. Perhaps the drawings were used as a type of calendar.

Petroglyphs may also be an expression of what the designer would want to see. For instance, consider the couple holding hands at McKee Spring. Was this the day of their marriage?

Some area Native American groups believe that shamans or medicine men would enter trances and have visions. They believe the images were already embedded in the rocks and that humans simply helped them out.

Bennis-Smith said that if she could be transported back in time, she'd ask the artists why they created a panel of spiral and concentric circles. "Why" she asks, "did they include anthropomorphs, concentric circles, and spirals all together?"

Whatever the case, Dinosaur preserves an incredible array of petroglyphs, and the McKee Spring panel offers one such exhibit. But don't confine yourself to the one panel—search out other petroglyphs, for each is intriguing in its own right. The following offers routes to some of the more easily located examples of rock art.

## McKee Spring

Take Brush Creek Road about 5 miles. Turn right on Island Park Road and proceed for 12 miles, reentering Dinosaur National Monument. McKee Spring is located about 3 miles beyond the park boundary along Island Park Road. If you drive another 5 miles, you will reach the Green River.

## Echo Park

Petroglyphs abound in and around the Echo Park area. Some are located on a rock ledge above the campground. The Pool Creek petroglyphs are located on the left about 0.5 mile before arriving at Echo Park Campground. Other petroglyphs are located directly across the Green River from the raft-launch site. Please remember that touching rock art or making rubbings corrodes the images and is an illegal activity.

To reach Echo Park, start at Headquarters Visitor Center (Colorado) on Harpers Corner Road. Travel 25.9 miles on Harpers Corner Road, then turn right at the sign for Echo Park Road. Go 9 miles. At the first T-junction, take the left-hand turn to Echo Park (there is a sign) for 4 more miles.

## Tour of the Tilted Rocks

To get to Tilted Rocks, use the western (Utah) entrance at the dinosaur quarry. In general, drive from the entrance station along the main road for about 5 miles, passing on your left the turnoff to the launch site and, 1 mile later, the turnoff to Green River Campground. Continue for about another mile, crossing the bridge over the Green River. From the bridge, proceed about 2 miles to a pullout. Here you will see a multitude of images. As is always the case, the most interesting drawings are reached with some effort. Follow the trail up the rather steep incline for about 200 yards until you reach the panel. Here you'll see a number of drawings of huge lizards.

*Bighorn sheep petroglyphs are numerous in Dinosaur National Monument.*

## Jones Hole Trail

You can access Jones Hole Trail by river or by car. If by river, hike up the trail that parallels Jones Hole Creek near the most upriver series of campsites. Hike for about 2 miles uphill to Ely Creek Campground. Continue past the campground for several hundred yards. On your left you will see a sign pointing to Deluge Shelter, which leads to the rock panel. The panel provides one of the most impressive groupings of pictographs in the monument.

To reach the same area by car—starting from the entrance station—follow the road out of the monument to Brush Creek Road. Follow Jones Hole Road for about 20 miles to the Jones Hole National Fish Hatchery. At the hatchery, follow the signs to the trailhead. From here, proceed down the trail for about 2 miles to the sign pointing to the Deluge Shelter. Turn right. A short hike will take you to the panel of pictographs. These pictographs are among the monument's most impressive. Look at the various forms, and once again you'll see what may be a shaman and bighorn sheep and a number of concentric circles.

## Mantle Cave

We accessed Mantle Cave on a four-day river trip down the Yampa River.

From the river, float about 200 yards past Mantle Ranch. Owners post their Internet address on a sign along the bank. Just downstream from the sign, beach your boat. Follow the well-delineated though unmarked trail through the brush, then uphill for about 0.5 mile to the cave's entrance.

Mantle Cave offers some rock art, but more impressive is the cave's huge structure, which once contained small granaries for food storage. Inside the cave, a trail takes you to several granaries, once used to safeguard corn. Look inside and you may see one small remaining ear. Once there were hundreds.

## Other Sites

Hundreds, possibly more than 1,000, other sites dot the monument, but you'll have to explore the backcountry and float the rivers to see them. Because of past vandalism, the park has elected not to delineate the location of all rock art or the considerable number of very impressive dwelling sites. We are following their lead. In a way this policy makes the discovery of a new panel more exciting, for you can believe with much justification that you are one of the few to have seen what you are seeing.

# Dinosaur's Bighorn Sheep

Of all of Dinosaur's seventy-some mammalian species, none is more conspicuous than the Rocky Mountain bighorn sheep. Elk are here, too, but they're more elusive—you seldom see them except in winter, when they herd up on various wintering grounds. But you'll see bighorns frequently, particularly if you float the Yampa and Green Rivers. Watch for them among the cliffs, where they move among the monument's ancient walls, securing themselves from their only real natural predator: the mountain lion.

Bighorn sheep have inhabited Dinosaur for more than 50,000 years, coping well with their several natural predators, such as the mountain lion, the eagle (on lambs), and the wolf. The only predator bighorn sheep could not tolerate was an unnatural one: man. Predictably, following the encroachment of civilization to the area in the late 1800s, the bighorns began to decline. By the early 1930s bighorn sheep had been extirpated—not so much from hunting as from the introduction of domestic sheep. Domestic sheep carry *Pasturella*, a disease that proved throughout the West to be more lethal than the combined effects of coyotes, golden eagles, cougars—or high-powered rifles.

But once bighorn sheep were abundant in Dinosaur National Monument. The country here offers an abundance of escape terrain, which serves as the biggest factor limiting their spread elsewhere. Now, thanks to the reintroduction efforts of various state game departments and the efforts of park biologists, the many bighorn trails used over the eons are being used again.

Because of various reintroductions, bighorn sheep in Dinosaur now number about 300 animals. Transplants first took place in the 1950s, and most recently in both 1997 and 1999. These recent transplants were made along the north face of Tank Peak and included twenty-one and twenty-seven animals, respectively. The animals were intended to augment existing herds, which are included in the 300 count. More transplants are anticipated, because park managers believe the monument has a carrying capacity of about 600.

Bighorn sheep are a fascinating mammalian species, and we are indeed lucky to have them in Dinosaur. Of all the ungulates, none has a more complex social system, and few have a more interesting life history. In late winter and in spring, look for herds consisting of rams, ewes, and lambs. In early June look along the cliff faces for single ewes. But if you see one, don't disturb her, as she may have just given birth to young.

Shortly after birthing, ewes will group together and form bands consisting of ewes and lambs. By this time, rams have departed the winter groups and have formed "bachelor" herds. Here they remain until the fall rut, at which time they become antagonistic toward one another, engaging in the battles for which they are so famous.

Floaters running the Green late in the year may well see these battles. So might those hiking the various park trails. One ranger reported seeing two rams engaged in a battle along Jones Hole Trail. The rams were so intent on subduing one another that they remained oblivious to the ranger's presence.

*Bighorn rams wear their autobiographies on their horns, which reveal past battles and current age.*

Bighorn rams have adapted to cranial collisions not only by the magnificent horns for which they are so well known but also by skull padding, nose padding, and sutures in their skulls that actually enable the bony plates protecting the brain to move. Together these adaptations enable rams to sustain blows of 2,400 foot-pounds of energy. Indeed, the forces of battle are considerable, and one biologist says the forces are additive.

Rams begin the contest by first rearing back, and from that point the forces begin to mount. Everything from the drop to the final lunge enters into the equation. After raising on hind legs, the two combatants begin dropping down, simultaneously charging. As the distance narrows, the rams lower their necks. Finally, they flick the horns forward and collide.

Rams often cease fighting after just one violent encounter, but not always. Many visitors have observed battles in which the contestants have blasted each other forty or more times in but a few short hours. In many cases, noses and skull get cracked. Sometimes battles continue to the death.

If you see any of these mountain monarchs—and you certainly will if you float the rivers or hike trails such as Jones Hole Trail—you should realize you are seeing an animal that evolved these capabilities in Asia almost a million years ago. About 50,000 years ago wild sheep crossed Beringia (part of the land strip between Alaska and Siberia, also known as the Bering Land Bridge National Preserve) and moved across the most desolate and barren lands of North America. As noted sheep biologist Valerius Geist explained, "Sheep have a fermentation vat that enabled them to process the grasses and other types of food materials typically found in dry dusty areas following such activities as glaciation."

Eventually populations came to inhabit most mountainous areas of the West, including the Uintas and, of course, Dinosaur. As park officials realized, bighorn sheep deserve to be here. Look to the numerous pictographs and petroglyphs on the walls, pecked and painted by the Fremont. Note how often the sheep motif occurs. Bighorn sheep have a long-standing history here, and when we see them we should proclaim ourselves fortunate.

Watch for bighorn sheep along both of the monument's rivers. Visitors often see several nice summer bands of "bachelor" rams along the Green several miles above the Split Mountain takeout. Watch, too, for bighorns along Jones Hole Trail.

## The Rivers: The Green and the Yampa

Perhaps the most effective way to explore Dinosaur is by watercraft, and there are two ways to do this. The easiest way—and certainly an extremely enjoyable way—is to join one of the park-endorsed raft companies that offers raft floats on both rivers, ranging in length from one to four days. The other way, of course, is to obtain your own permit and use your personal raft, kayak, or canoe.

River travel gives a new perspective to the wonders of Dinosaur National Monument. Geology, history, flora, and fauna—all are seen close-up and personal from the water, in a way not possible from the top of the canyons. River campgrounds are well spaced, large, and clean. Each river has something unique to offer its travelers. The Yampa River is the last free-flowing river in the Colorado River system; the Green River is dammed at Flaming Gorge Reservoir.

We have floated the monument's two rivers on our own and with a raft company; we can assure you that each way has its own merits. If you have the proven experience, and if you can obtain a permit, you can run either the Green or the Yampa on your own. You cannot, however, run both rivers in the same year on your own.

Normally you should begin the application process for a permit sometime in the fall, well in advance of a spring or summer float. We were extraordinarily lucky. We applied in March for a permit to run the Green, and good fortune certainly did smile our way. Just moments before our call, a party had canceled, and we immediately provided a credit-card deposit. Others have gone a year or more before acquiring a permit. Several parties told us they had finally obtained a permit only by using the speed-dial capability on their phone and had repeatedly pushed those buttons for hours.

Chapter 10 (Exploring Dinosaur National Monument by River, page 81) gives more detailed information on the rivers of Dinosaur and running them.

## Driving Tour 1: Tour of the Tilted Rocks

**LENGTH:** 22 miles round-trip.

**ROAD CONDITIONS:** Good paved road, except for the last 2 miles, which are dirt and may be impassable when wet.

**TIME NEEDED:** 1½ to 2 hours.

**MAPS:** 50-cent brochure by Dinosaur National Monument; National Geographic Trails Illustrated Map #220.

**STARTING POINT:** Coming from the west (from the entrance gate at the dinosaur quarry), just past the left turn for the quarry, you'll see a box on the south side of the road containing guide booklets (50 cents) for this tour. Stop 1 is about 1 mile east of the quarry. The Quarry Visitor Center bookstore and Headquarters Visitor Center (in Colorado) also carry these pamphlets.

**TAKE ALONG:** Water, hat, sunscreen, and perhaps a picnic for road's end.

**Summary of the drive:** The Tour of the Tilted Rocks (see map on page 24 of this chapter) is an excellent introduction to the many facets of Dinosaur National Monument. Many visitors tour the quarry first and then drive this short auto tour. There are interpretive signs and short walks along the way, so you're not always stuck in a vehicle. The route has fifteen numbered stops and two short enjoyable hikes at the end.

Sights to be seen begin with the Swelter Shelter, an alcove once used by Paleo-Indian and Fremont people. Here you can view both pictographs and petroglyphs made by the Fremont people perhaps 1,000 years ago. If you visit in the heat of the day, you'll see why archaeologists called this the Swelter Shelter when they were excavating the area.

As you travel down the road, the beauty and phenomenon of Split Mountain and the Green River unfold before you. The tour takes you down to Split Mountain boat ramp and campground. Near the boat ramp you can hike (recommended) the 2-mile Desert Voices Nature Trail (see Chapter 7, Nature Hikes, page 46).

Leaving Split Mountain, the road climbs above Green River Campground, providing a great view of the winding Green River. Then the road leaves the

*Swelter Shelter.*

monument briefly and winds by the privately owned Chew family ranch. At Stop 10, look for Turtle Rock on the left side of the road, formed from Entrada sandstone.

At Mile 10, take the left fork and cross Cub Creek. Here the road becomes dirt/gravel. At Stop 13, Mile 10.6, on the north side of the road, look for groups of petroglyphs on the rocks above. The drawings stand out better when the light is subdued. Walk up the paths to the rocks to view them and wonder just what the artist was trying to say in his rock stories. Two-tenths of a mile farther (Mile 10.8), if the light is right you'll see huge lizard drawings on the dark desert varnish of the walls above. We strongly recommend this short hike, for there are many smaller petroglyphs here as well.

Farther down the road (no pullout), look to the low rocks on the left to see what is known as the Three Princesses. The National Park Service asks that you not touch the drawings—they are fragile and valuable both historically and aesthetically. Human skin contains oils, which will corrode the images.

The old homestead of Josephine Bassett Morris provides the final stop (15) and is affectionately known as Josie's Cabin. The buildings are still standing, and if you spend a little time, you'll learn the story of a rugged individualist who chose to live in this beautiful canyon area alone for nearly fifty years. Josie hunted, raised fruit and vegetables, kept livestock, and had no modern conveniences. She simply loved solitude, and here she found it.

You can take one or both of the two short hikes leading from Josie's Cabin. Both Hog Canyon and Box Canyon walks (see Chapter 8, Hiking Trails, page 67) are level and mostly shaded. It was in these canyons that Josie used the natural barriers to pen her livestock—just one example of this lady's ingenuity.

Water flows here. Various kinds of trees and wildflowers flourish, all encapsulated by the towering walls of the surrounding canyons. In 1987 botanists found a rare orchid, *Spiranthes diluvialis*, growing in a meadow at Josie's on the trail to Hog Canyon. An interpretive sign says in part, ". . . in this small piece of the universe is a beauty that represents diversity and stability." Watercress grows profusely along the creek bottoms. As well, there are many mint plants, yarrow, sage, wild rose and bee plants.

Under the shade trees next to Josie's Cabin are picnic tables. The water from the stream is not recommended for drinking, so be sure to carry some with you. Return via the same road.

# Tour of the Tilted Rocks, Harpers Corner Scenic Drive, Plug Hat Trail, and Harpers Corner Trail

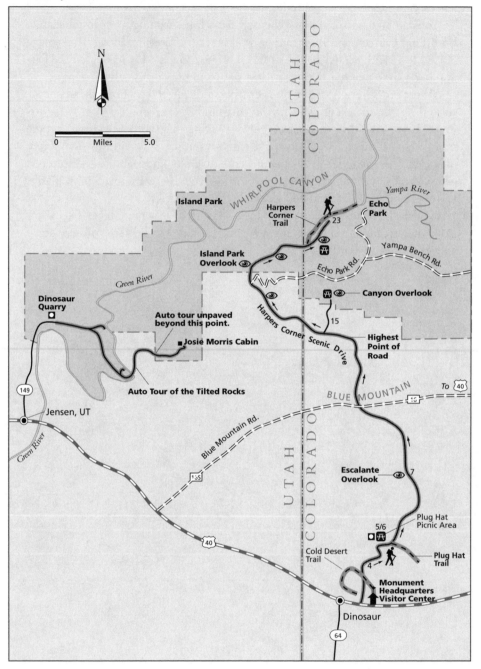

# Driving Tour 2:
# Harpers Corner Scenic Drive: Journey through Time

**LENGTH:** 64 miles round-trip, with a 2-mile optional hike at the end.

**ROAD CONDITIONS:** Paved road the entire way. No facilities on the road. Pit toilets at picnic areas and overlooks.

**TIME NEEDED:** At least half a day.

**MAPS:** *Journey through Time* guide, from Intermountain Natural History Association (50 cents); National Geographic Trails Illustrated Map #220; *Harpers Corner Trail Guide* from Intermountain Natural History Association (25 cents).

**STARTING POINT:** At Monument Headquarters Visitor Center in Colorado, 25 miles east of Jensen, Utah, on U.S. Highway 40. The entrance is on the north side of the road, 2 miles east of the town of Dinosaur, Colorado. Guidebooks for the road tour and trail are available here or at Dinosaur Quarry Visitor Center.

**TAKE ALONG:** Water, hat, sunscreen, bug spray, camera, and perhaps a picnic.

**Summary of the drive:** This driving tour is intended to introduce visitors to the canyon country of the monument, along the Green and Yampa Rivers. No dinosaur fossils are available for viewing in this area, and camping is not allowed along the route. As you'll see from your map, most of the drive is actually in Colorado, outside the monument. The road crosses into Utah and finally, at Mile 27.5, enters the park and reenters Colorado.

The drive offers twenty-three numbered stops, all of which provide excellent interpretation of the canyons, formations, trees, and plants of the area.

The first short, easy, 0.5-mile walk on the tour leaves from just behind the visitor center and is called the Cold Desert Hike. This very informative hike explains how certain plants and animals exist in this arid high-desert ecosystem located at the edge of the Great Basin Desert (see Chapter 7, Nature Hikes, page 51).

Another highlight is Plug Hat Trail (0.5 mile) at Stop 5. The level stroll offers a panorama of the Colorado Plateau and, in the distance, views of the Morrison Formation, famous as a repository of dinosaur fossils.

As you drive, note the vast amount of sagebrush (a haven for the sage grouse). Note also the grazing sheep and cattle. In spring, arrow-leaf balsamroot plants light up the hills with their yellow blooms. Once they provided a beacon for Indians, who dug and subsisted on their roots.

*Steamboat Rock, along the Green River at historic Echo Park.*

At about Mile 16.5 you reach the highest point on the road. A small stand of quaking aspen appears on the north-facing hill.

At Stop 17 the high Uinta Mountains run east to west, at times spiraling to more than 13,000 feet in height. From the same vantage along the drive you can also see Zenobia Peak—at 9,006 feet the highest elevation in Dinosaur National Monument. In summer the peak hosts a manned fire tower.

Stop 18 shows privately owned corrals. The area was once the stomping grounds of such outlaws and rustlers as Butch Cassidy and the Sundance Kid. The old Outlaw Trail, where stolen cattle were driven and thieves hid out, passed near here.

Mile 25.9 is the turnoff for Echo Park Road. Heed the sign: PASSENGER CARS NOT ADVISED. NO TRAILERS. IMPASSABLE WHEN WET. Continue on Harpers Corner Road here, if time is a consideration. Echo Park Road is only 13 miles long, but it is rough and unpaved, and it takes the better part of an hour to drive one-way. (See Chapter 6, Backcountry Driving Tours, page 31, for a more complete description of Echo Park Road.)

Stop 20 (Mile 28.3) is Island Park Overlook and the trailhead for Ruple Point Trail, an 8-mile out-and-back hike offering views at the end.

At Stop 22, Echo Park Overlook, look below for the junction of the Green and Yampa Rivers. Look, too, for Steamboat Rock, standing 700 feet above the Green. Echo Park was the scene of great controversy in the 1950s, as one of the proposed dam sites was just downriver from Echo Park and would have flooded the entire area. If that had come to pass, the canyons with their beauty and rock art would have been underwater, the plants and animals gone.

Stop 23 at Mile 32 is the end of the road. From the parking lot you can access the start of Harpers Corner Trail, a 2-mile out-and-back hike of moderate difficulty (partly because of the 7,500-foot elevation). If time permits, this trail should not be missed, as the views and photographic opportunities (early and late in the day) are incredible (see Chapter 7, Nature Hikes, page 55).

If you drive Harpers Corner Road in the summer months, you may well be treated to a most unusual phenomenon—the infamous Mormon crickets, first fought by farmers long ago in Salt Lake City. Not a cricket at all, these rather ugly, large bugs are actually wingless grasshoppers. They eat their way across the desert environment, seeking protein in order to lay their eggs. Long the bane of ranchers and farmers, the insects seem to appear in six- to seven-year cycles, much like the dreaded seven-year locusts.

We drove the road several times during the month of June and were amazed at the sight of the bugs swarming all over the road, making the asphalt shimmer and appear to be swaying. Many insects had been run over by vehicles, and their relatives were having a feeding frenzy. We stopped and realized the vegetation on either side of the road was also swarming with Mormon crickets.

Because they are wingless, Mormon crickets must be somewhat inventive in their mode of travel. We saw them swimming the Green River and hitching rides on any river craft that came along. They are curious-looking creatures and have an interesting life history.

# The Mormon Cricket

With its black elongated body, large eyes, short wings, and dark coloration, the Mormon cricket may be a candidate for one of North America's ugliest bugs. What's more, when you see one, you usually see thousands. Sometimes that adds to their ugly-bug persona.

We first saw Mormon crickets the way most see them: squashed and ground into the road by the thousands. When we ran over them, as we had to on our drive to Harpers Corner, filaments of their bodies got flung into the recesses of our wheel wells, where the rotting pieces soon engulfed our truck with a stench that persisted. Based on these first introductions, it came as a shock to us to learn that some early settlers would eat the insects, learning about their survival value from Native Americans. It may also come as a surprise that for us, following repeated encounters, the cricket became an object of great fascination.

Despite their designation as crickets, entomologists say the bug is really a wingless longhorn grasshopper. But mid-nineteenth-century Mormon settlers, more concerned about the quality of their first crops, could not have cared less. They called them a cricket, and the name stuck. Judging from the magnitude of their numbers, they may well have called them by other names, too. In actuality, today's Mormon crickets are cousins of the grasshopper horde that attacked the Mormon farmers.

*The infamous Mormon cricket.*

Little wonder that the men and women who witnessed this invasion gave thanks to the flocks of seagulls that descended onto infested fields about that same time and feasted on the crickets, saving those first of Mormon crops.

If you're confronted with an infestation of "crickets," you might think you're seeing every existing cricket because of their sheer magnitude. In reality, crickets are widespread, and you might see them at the same time others are seeing plagues in Minnesota, Oregon, or states in between—or even in some of Canada's western provinces. Many believe such masses of crickets can totally denude an area, but researchers say such is not likely, at least when a plant community—including croplands—is in a healthy condition.

Studies have shown that crickets are nibblers, rarely eating a plant to the ground. Studies have also shown that crickets prefer to eat broad-leafed plants such as arrow-leaf balsamroot, lupine, and loco-weed. Because crickets migrate, their effect on an area is temporary. Fortunately they seem to be cyclical invaders, showing up perhaps every two or five to seven years.

But over the decades such knowledge has been of little consolation, and residents have frequently attempted to squelch the insects' march. They have used poisons, barriers of 15-inch-high sheet iron, pits, and other ingenious techniques to foil the bugs' movement. More recently scientists have developed a biological control, but the parasite has not proven to be very effective.

If you're interested in finding Mormon crickets (for whatever reason), Dinosaur National Monument just might be your mecca. During the summer that we were collecting information for this book, we saw them in many places. Once we saw them as we floated the Green River. Another day we saw them in hordes along the road to Harpers Corner—there we were so fascinated by such overwhelming examples of biomass that we simply had to have a closer look.

Mormon crickets are, in fact, intriguing. Watch them as they stream across the landscape. You may be watching the progression of a band numbering more than a million. Entomologists say that before summer's end, your band may travel 25 to 30 miles.

Watch them, too, as they feed on their deceased comrades—and then try and refrain from such anthropomorphisms as "ghoulish." Biologists say the crickets need this protein in order to lay their eggs.

Biologically, Mormon crickets are interesting because of their unusual sexual behavior. During mating males attempt to attract females, but unlike most other species, when male and female come together, it's the female that mounts the male rather than vice versa.

Researchers believe that males are highly selective. When a male accepts a female, he transfers to her a spermatophore, which can amount to 30 percent of his body weight. The spermatophore is a sac that attaches to the female's abdomen. In it are sperm ampules, protein, and nutrients intended to help the female.

Shortly after mating, females deposit eggs in the ground using a long saber-like ovipositor. Eggs lay dormant through the fall and until the first winter thaw. If the thaw is too early—February, for example—the eggs start to hatch. Then, if winter returns—as it generally does—most of the eggs die. But if the ground remains frozen throughout winter and into spring, the eggs hatch and the "crickets" generally survive. That explains why some years produce such bumper crops of crickets.

Regardless of numbers, the process of growth begins in spring, progressing through seven molts. If the population of crickets is large enough, they band together, generally by the second or third molt. By early June they are adults and are ready to move.

In the past, Native Americans knew such numbers represented food and would gather the bugs in baskets, scooping them from rivers, which the crickets would sometimes use as corridors of migration. Today we might wrinkle our noses, but don't we consider chocolate-covered grasshoppers a delicacy? Essentially they're not much different from a Mormon cricket, just a different color.

Anyone want us to pass a cricket?

# Chapter 6
# Backcountry Driving Tours

## Backcountry Driving Tour 1:
## Echo Park Road and Mitten Park Hike

**LENGTH:** 13 miles one-way.

**ROAD CONDITIONS:** Poor (rutted) dirt/gravel road. Best for four-wheel-drive or high-clearance vehicles. The road is impassable when wet and is often closed under these conditions. It is open only in summer and fall.

**TIME NEEDED:** 1 hour driving time each way. Plan to spend nearly a full day exploring, or plan to camp in the lovely Echo Park Campground ($6.00 per night, seventeen tent sites, five walk-ins and one group site; water, vault toilets, tables, fireplaces; no RVs or trailers). If time permits, plan to hike beautiful Mitten Park Trail, which departs from Echo Park Campground behind the group camping site.

**MAPS:** Dinosaur National Monument handout map; National Geographic Trails Illustrated Map #220.

**STARTING POINT:** Headquarters Visitor Center (Colorado) on Harpers Corner Road. Travel 25.9 miles on Harpers Corner Road, then turn right at the sign for Echo Park Road. Go 9 miles. At the first T-junction, take the left-hand turn to Echo Park (there is a sign) for 4 more miles. The right-hand turn will take you onto Yampa Bench Road.

**TAKE ALONG:** Hat, layered clothing, water (available in summer at Echo Park Campground), sunscreen, bug spray, food.

**Summary of the drive:** From its description this road sounds a bit ominous. Generally, however, it's not that rough, and it is spectacular scenically and historically. It is also one of the few roads in the monument from which the Green and Yampa Rivers can be accessed and their shores explored on foot. Sometimes rafters use the road as a takeout from the Green River. With a permit, others use it as a river put-in point for multiday river trips only. If you drive slowly, Echo Park Road becomes another backcountry adventure. Note the monument sign at the entrance to the road cautioning PASSENGER CARS NOT ADVISED. NO TRAILERS. IMPASSABLE WHEN WET. If you disregard the cautionary sign, the road

*Echo Park Road*

could become a real adventure—there are steep switchbacks for the first 2 miles.

As you start down the road, you'll notice the red rocks and the dirt. This is part of the Moenkopi Formation. When wet, it metamorphoses into a surface that acts like greased ball bearings. In the early 1900s the Chew family operated a ranch nearly at the end of the present road. They drove their wagon teams straight down this steep hillside. When they returned it was a two- to three-day trip back up to town by horse and buggy.

From the twisting, turning start, wonderful vistas open. You pass rock formations that intrigue geologists. Towering formations and large caves of Weber sandstone (wind-deposited granules) tell you something of the force of wind in the tortuous canyon. Our first night in Echo Park Campground the wind gusted so violently that it deposited layers of fine-grained sand in our tent through tiny openings. We were lucky—the wind toppled other tents.

Besides the pleasure of driving the road, there's much to do at Echo Park (called a "park" simply because it is an open area in a land of canyons). After passing the old, now-abandoned Chew Ranch, you'll see a sign for Pool Creek petroglyphs on your left, pecked out long ago by the Fremont people.

About a mile farther down the road, the chill of Whispering Caves invites a stop. As you walk to the cave you feel the rush of cool air before you get to the entrance. The cave is very narrow and difficult to explore, but it is an interesting phenomenon. The entrance to Echo Park Campground is now just down the road on the left.

Echo Park is the location of the confluence of the Yampa and Green Rivers. The road ends at the Green River, about 0.25 mile below the confluence, reached by continuing but a short distance beyond the campground. Often you'll hear boaters shouting as they come through to hear the echoes for which the place is famous. The area is also the end of Lodore Canyon and the beginning of Whirlpool Canyon on the Green River.

## Mitten Park Hike

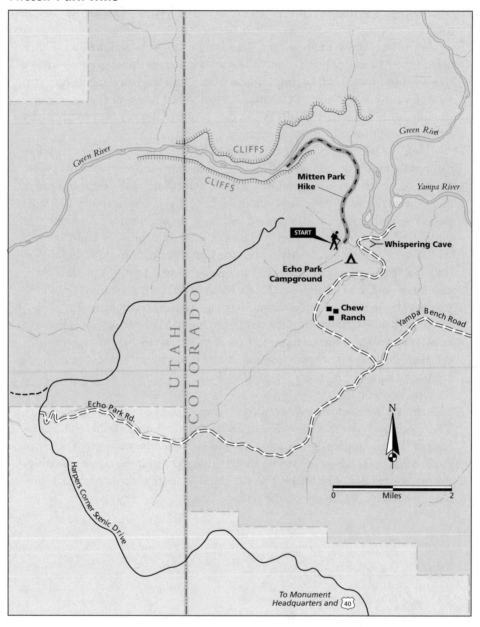

## Mitten Park Hike

**TYPE OF TRAIL:** In and out.

**TOTAL DISTANCE:** 1.5 miles round-trip.

**ELEVATION CHANGE:** 400 feet.

**TIME REQUIRED:** Approximately 1½ hours.

**DIFFICULTY:** Moderate.

**STARTING POINT:** From behind the walk-in campsite at Echo Park Campground.

**The hike:** Mitten Park Trail is accessed from Echo Park Campground. On summer weekends park rangers often lead a walk on this trail, and they offer good interpretations. Check at one of the visitor centers for the weekly hand-out on ranger programs. If you miss one of these, walk the trail anyway. The views of the Green River and Mitten Park Fault shouldn't be missed.

*Whispering Cave on Echo Park Road.*

## Echo Park

The petroglyphs in Echo Park were made sometime between 750 and 1,800 years ago. If you chance upon some of this incredible art, allow your imagination to expand a bit. Why did Indians take the time to climb the steep walls, using handholds that are no longer present? Were they trying to improve the fertility of the sheep? Were bighorn sheep dying out from the canyon and, if so, were the artists trying to lure them back using the magic of rock art?

Obviously no one will ever know, but what we do know is that this small part of Echo Park was almost engulfed by the immense floodwaters that would have resulted from the construction of yet another dam on the Colorado River drainage system.

Back in the 1950s dam builders sought an increase of water levels for irrigation and hydroelectric power. Proponents of the time used psychological ploys, ones that attempted to make the opposition feel guilty.

"These scenic gorges and primitive areas were withdrawn from the recreation of the people," said one developer. "No true conservationist would oppose a project that would make them easier and safer to reach."

Had the developers succeeded, water levels would have risen 500 feet. Those who favored development said conservationists must compromise, but what they failed to explain was that there was nothing left to compromise— every river in the Colorado River drainage was about to be dammed or already had been. Little wonder that the fight to save Echo Park became a battle. Today hydrological charts show those results in a most dramatic fashion. Where once a steady flow of water poured into the Gulf of Mexico, today at times there is nothing more than a trickle.

Fortunately strong conservation forces obtained support when they challenged the government's right to dam a national monument, or there might not be even a trickle. The National Park Service and the Sierra Club held that the National Park Act of 1916 forbade any infringement on the right of the public and of future generations to enjoy the area.

By itself, obliteration of the panel of petroglyphs may not have been that significant to some. But when you realize that the waters would have flooded most portions of the Yampa that flow through Dinosaur and almost all the Green upstream from Echo Park to the Canyon of Lodore—that it would have flooded out other rock art, considerable history, and incomparable beauty—the impact assumes even more horrendous proportions.

But construction of the dam site represented the thinking of the times, and because some of that thinking seems to be cropping up again, it is important to remember that Echo Park—perhaps more than any other site in North America—embodies some of the early beginnings of the movement to save beautiful places, the conservation movement as it is known today. Echo Park also serves

*Ranger-led hike on Mitten Park Trail at Echo Park.*

to remind us what groups of people who believe in preservation can do when they put aside petty squabbles and unite.

Echo Park, like no other issue, attracted people from many walks of life. It brought photographers and writers together. The dam controversy gave birth to the conservation movement, which became a political force with which to be reckoned. It provided the Sierra Club with David Brower, a strong leader whose voice will undoubtedly live long past his demise.

With single-minded intent, Brower raised the cause of Echo Park to a national battle cry. Though he later lamented having been forced to sacrifice Glen Canyon in compromise for Echo Park, many still believe the decision was the correct one.

Today it may be difficult to believe that these canyons were almost dammed. But never forget that developers once eyed these areas—and still do. As you pass Steamboat Rock, explore Whispering Cave, find a secret midden, or even hike into Mantle Cave, remember that none of this would exist had it not been for the work of farsighted men and women who believed that Echo Park contained something priceless.

# Backcountry Driving Tour 2: Yampa Bench Road

**LENGTH:** Yampa Bench Road is 27 miles long one-way. However, you must drive almost 26 miles up Harpers Corner Scenic Drive Road, then 8 miles down Echo Park Road, for a total of almost 61 miles (excluding the mileage from your starting point).

**ROAD CONDITIONS:** The road is unpaved and very rough in places, especially around Hells Canyon. It is best for four-wheel-drive or high-clearance vehicles. The road is impassable when wet.

**TIME NEEDED:** 4 to 5 hours, but give this trip a full day for stops, walks, photo opportunities, and just plain exploring.

**MAPS:** Free map of area, available at Monument Headquarters; National Geographic Trails Illustrated Map #220.

**STARTING AND EXIT POINT:** Go 25.9 miles up Harpers Corner Scenic Drive to the right-hand turnoff for Echo Park Road. Take Echo Park Road for 8 miles to a T-junction. Go right onto Yampa Bench Road. At the end of the road trip, on Blue Mountain, is a junction. Turn right onto County Roads 95 and 16, which take you back to U.S. Highway 40. You are now about 24 miles east of Monument Headquarters. You can also turn left at the junction and access County Road 14. This also takes you back to U.S. 40 at Elk Springs, which is about 32 miles east of Monument Headquarters. Obviously you can turn around and retrace the drive at any point.

**TAKE ALONG:** Water, camera, food, sunscreen, sturdy shoes (and be sure to gas up your vehicle).

**Summary of the drive:** Like its neighboring road, Echo Park, Yampa Bench Road is worth the effort, and your time is well spent on this trip into the heart of Dinosaur National Monument. We decided that the road conditions may well depend on the time of year and whether a road grader has been through the area. On the day of our drive, we found Yampa Bench Road to be in surprisingly good condition; it was only rough and rocky ascending Hells Canyon. The road parallels the Yampa River the entire way, quite high above it on the towering cliffs. There are five designated pullouts where you can park and wander out to the overlooks for some incredible views and beautiful photo opportunities.

The first stop (in about 3.5 miles) is Castle Park Overlook on the left side of the road. You need to look carefully for the sign, as it is not large. The land below you belongs to the Mantle family; they have ranched here since 1919. Believe it or not, directly below in the canyon to the right is Mantle Cave,

## Yampa Bench Road

*The Yampa River from Harding Hole Overlook.*

which can be accessed from the river, if you are on one of the guided multiday trips or if you're floating on your own. A sandy beach offers a good landing spot, and then it's about a 0.5-mile walk up to the cave.

Mantle Cave is actually a huge—really huge—alcove, used in prehistoric times by the Fremont people as a storage area for corn or other items they wanted to preserve. Excavated in the 1940s, most of the artifacts are now stored at the University of Colorado, but the circular stone storage bins remain. Even on the hottest day, the alcove is cool and welcoming. Bats have made the cave their home.

Leaving this stop, you enter Hells Canyon; at the fork, take a right. If you continue straight, you'll be on private land and a private road. After a steep, rough climb with switchbacks, you come to Harding Hole Overlook on the left. Do stop here; the view of the winding Yampa River and the formations is spectacular.

The next stop is Wagon Wheel Overlook, which offers more beautiful views. You can see campsites below, used by today's river runners.

The road now swings a bit away from the river, bringing you to the Baker Cabin stop, which is on the right. An abandoned homestead, it makes one realize the toughness of the ranchers who once chose to live out here.

The last pullout is Haystack Rock Overlook on the left. If you are visiting between April and mid-July, you'll find the road out to the overlook is closed. Peregrine falcons have been reintroduced to their native habitat here, and this is a prime nesting site. No visitors means no disturbance for these beautiful and easily disturbed birds.

At the tour's end you begin the ascent up Blue Mountain and soon reach the monument's boundary. Follow the above directions to return to US 40.

## Nature Hike 1: Sound of Silence Hiking Route

**TYPE OF TRAIL:** Self-guided loop route.

**TOTAL DISTANCE:** Approximately 2.5 miles.

**ELEVATION CHANGE:** 100 to 150 feet; there are sections of short, steep descents.

**TIME REQUIRED:** 2 to 3 hours.

**MAPS:** Intermountain Natural History Association pamphlet.

**DIFFICULTY:** Moderate, with a few short, steep ascents and descents.

**STARTING POINT:** From the turnoff (on your left) to the dinosaur quarry, stay straight (east) on Cub Creek Road. Continue past the Swelter Shelter for a short distance until you see the trailhead sign on the left. *NOTE:* Dogs and bikes are not allowed on the trail.

**The hike:** Sound of Silence is not intended to be a marked hiking trail. It is referred to as a *route* and is intended to challenge you to find your way around this loop (clockwise). It is designed as a lesson in minimum-impact desert hiking so that you might feel more comfortable hiking farther at another time. Arrows are placed at strategic locations, helping to guide you to each of the twenty-six numbered markers. If you pay close attention, you won't get lost! You can purchase (for 50 cents) an excellent interpretive pamphlet, either at the trailhead box or at the dinosaur quarry bookstore. This publication is not only informative, it is your guide on the route. As you begin the hike, you are 1 mile above sea level.

Before starting out, consider some important facts. If you suffer from respiratory conditions or have a heart problem, you should take it easy. Try this route early in the morning to avoid the midday desert heat, and carry lots of water. A few ups and downs are rather steep; wear good shoes, and don't attempt these areas if you have knee or leg problems. After Marker 10 the path becomes somewhat more difficult; for some, this might be a good place to turn back. If you get off the path, try at all costs to avoid stepping on the black microbiotic soil. The best areas to place your feet are in the sandy washes or on bare rock. Finally, remember the name of this hike and listen for the sound of silence.

# Sound of Silence Hiking Route

Sound of Silence Hiking Route

RIDGE

To Desert Voices Nature Trail

ANFRACTUOSITY

SAND CLIFFS

RED WASH

CLIFFS

Marker 2

START

Trailhead

P

N

Swelter Shelter

To Dinosaur Quarry, Geology Trail and Visitor Center

Cub Creek Road

0.9

To Split Mountain Campground

0    Mile    0.5

As you begin the route, it appears that you are heading straight for jumbles of huge rocks, which you are. For a while you'll be hiking down the soft sands of Red Wash—actually, for nearly half the hike. Soon a large cottonwood tree comes into view. This means that the water table here must be close to the surface, but you'd never guess that from the dryness surrounding you. The next indicators of water are tamarisk bushes, a nonnative water usurper. This plant has become a major problem in many parts of Dinosaur, as it robs native plants of the much-needed liquid.

Farther along, sage bushes become numerous, as do lichen-covered rocks. There are some cottonwoods in the wash. Look carefully and you'll probably see rabbit, elk, or perhaps mule deer droppings. If you're lucky, you'll catch a glimpse of the animal itself.

At Marker 11 the route enters a sort of maze; stay right. Before long there will be a small area where juniper trees provide a shady rest. View the white rocks of Split Mountain to the north and think about how old they are.

After Marker 13 we spotted a few prickly pear cacti along the ridge, but only a few. Before turning uphill at Marker 15, we again rested under some junipers. The views in this area are dramatic. Continue on, and use caution when going up or down the sandstone rocks. They can be slippery, especially when wet.

Near Marker 25 we found a small group of thin-leaf yucca plants. It was the first time we'd seen this plant in the monument. Marker 26 is last on the route. Just beyond Marker 26 is Red Wash. Turn left in the wash to Marker 2, and return to your vehicle.

*Sound of Silence Hiking Route.*

# Desert Voices Nature Trail and Geology Trail

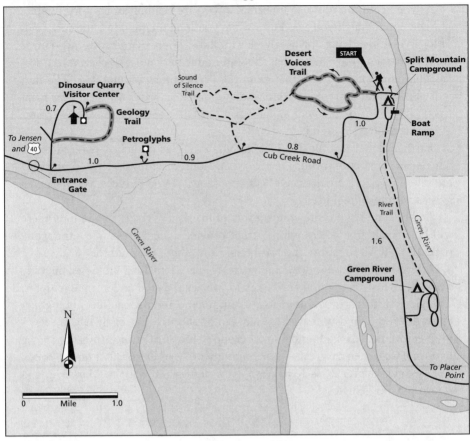

# Nature Hike 2: Desert Voices Nature Trail

**TYPE OF TRAIL:** Self-guided loop.

**TOTAL DISTANCE:** 2 miles.

**ELEVATION CHANGE:** 500 feet.

**TIME REQUIRED:** 1 to 2 hours.

**MAPS:** Intermountain Natural History Association pamphlet; National Geographic Trails Illustrated Map #220.

**DIFFICULTY:** Moderately strenuous; however, the difficulty rating increases in hot weather or if you're hiking in the heat of the day. Try this one in early morning or late afternoon.

**STARTING POINT:** Split Mountain boat ramp and campground area. The Split Mountain boat ramp is located approximately 2.4 miles east of the dinosaur quarry. Follow the paved road from the quarry to the first left-hand turn down to the Split Mountain boat ramp and campground. The trailhead is across from the boat ramp on the left. Park in the lot on the right. We walked in a counterclockwise direction.

**TAKE ALONG:** Water, hat, camera, and sunscreen.

**The hike:** Desert Voices Nature Trail provides a 2-mile hike through the desert environment and offers excellent views of famous Split Mountain. If you are hiking the trail late on a well-lit summer day, watch how the sun seems to separate Split Mountain into two units. To learn more about the unique geological features of the mountain, see Chapter 1 (Overview of Dinosaur National Monument, page 1). This moderately strenuous hike offers interpretations of a number of unique desert aspects. And because many of the signs and pictures along the route were created by children (the tan signs), this is a good trek on which to include young people.

Consider the moving insights of August Teague, age 12: I DREW THE MARIPOSA LILY BECAUSE I MISSED MY MOM AND MY MOM LOVES FLOWERS. IT WAS THE PRETTIEST FLOWER THAT I EVER SAW, AND MAYBE THE PRETTIEST THAT I WILL EVER SEE.

The mariposa lily is a common flower in season along this trail, and indeed it is one of the prettiest. Like all other lilies, it is characterized by the floral formula of three sepals, three petals, six stamen, and three pistils. A large dark spot at the base of each of its petals further identifies it.

If you are new to desert environments, this trail will introduce you to the features of one of four North American deserts: the Great Basin Desert, which is classified as a high desert. The number and proliferation of cacti here is far less when compared with other deserts, such as the Sonoran or Mojave, which

*Desert Voices Nature Trail.*

are close to the Great Basin. One interpretive sign explains much: IN DESERTS EVAPORATION EXCEEDS RAINFALL.

One particularly interesting explanation provided by the walk is an introduction to cryptogamic or microbiotic soil, easily recognized by its black coloration. Biologists explain that this very fragile soil is a living plant community consisting of fungi, algae, and often moss or bacterial colonies. In nature this substance is important, as it helps hold moisture in the ground to be used by other plants. When its components die and break down, the soil serves as a fertilizer for other plants. It also helps keep soil from being washed away by rain and wind. Without it some other plant species would find existence more difficult. As you hike, heed the caution signs to remain on the trail and avoid walking on the cryptogamic soil.

Along the trail you'll come upon an explanation for lichens. In the monument you'll see many varieties of lichen of many colors, and there's a reason. The brightness of the lichen is an indicator of air quality, and from what we observed, the air quality in Dinosaur National Monument is quite good indeed.

The trail meanders up and down, with the steepest part at the top, just before you begin the downward half of the loop. Take time to read all the interpretive signs to increase your understanding of this amazing place. Some signs interpret creatures you are likely to see. Look at the two species of lizards, for example, and watch as they engage in what appear to be push-ups. Feel the heat from the desert floor at midday, and you'll realize that the lizards elevate themselves off the ground with their legs to keep cool. You may catch sight of mule deer and rabbits on your hike. These animals have evolved for desert living with longer extremities than their counterparts in colder climes. Their long ears have blood vessels running close to the surface to help dissipate heat. The prairie dog burrows beneath the ground into the cooler earth. If you're quiet, you may also see an occasional fox or coyote. Dinosaur is also home to a number of rare, threatened, and endangered species of plants and animals, and from this trail you may see them. Across the way toward Split Mountain, peregrine falcons sometimes nest on the sheer cliffs. Watch for them.

As you proceed farther along the walk, other examples of children's thoughts are provided. Here are a few:

> The heat and power of the sun rules the desert.
>
> —YANU VALENTINE, AGE 12

> All the different grasses I saw. How the look and feel of the environment would change without them.
>
> —MARIAH BAUER, AGE 13

> When there is nothing but wilderness around you and only the stars or a setting sun giving light, it's very easy to believe in yourself.
>
> —AMANDA HEDDEN

There are places along the trail to sit on rocks and a few places to get out of the sun. This is a must-do hike, which shows great examples of high-desert life. As mentioned earlier, the National Park Service categorizes the trail as moderately strenuous, but the difficulty increases in summer, when temperatures often exceed 100 degrees Fahrenheit. At this time of year, the trail would be categorized as strenuous because it ascends continuously for about half its distance. As always when hiking in the desert, carry water (lots), use sunscreen, and wear a good hat.

## Cold Desert Trail

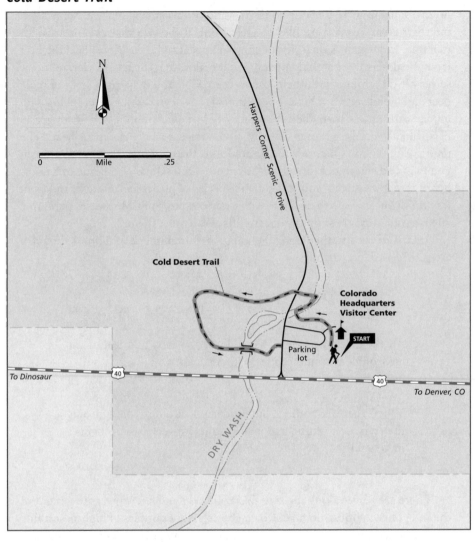

# Nature Hike 3: Cold Desert Trail

**TYPE OF TRAIL:** Self-guided nature loop.

**TOTAL DISTANCE:** 0.25 mile.

**ELEVATION CHANGE:** None.

**TIME REQUIRED:** 15 minutes to 1 hour.

**MAPS:** Intermountain Natural History Association booklet, available in box by trail.

**DIFFICULTY:** Very easy.

**STARTING POINT:** The trailhead begins at the south side of the parking lot of the visitor center, which is the first right turn after you enter Harpers Corner Scenic Drive. From Jensen, Utah, take U.S. Highway 40 east toward Colorado for 25 miles. You will see the sign for Dinosaur Monument Headquarters and Visitor Center. Take a left at this point off US 40. The visitor center and trail are just up Harpers Corner Scenic Road on the right.

**The hike:** If you're exploring the Cold Desert Trail on a July day, you may disagree with the designation of this 0.25-mile-long path. "Cold Desert," however, is apt. The trail is located at an elevation of about 6,000 feet, and the monument itself is located in a more northern latitude. Therefore the term *cold* is appropriate. But the term *desert* is also correct. The trail is located on the lee side of the Wasatch Range and receives very little moisture. How does life adapt to such extremes? In part that's what this hike explains. But the hike offers more. Because of a flash flood in 1999, the hike provides insights into the effects of sudden and heavy water in an area that normally receives only 6 to 8 inches of rain over the span of an entire year.

The flood occurred on the afternoon of 31 July 1999, when a thunderstorm unleashed 0.5 inch of rain in less than 20 minutes. In a few minutes, millions of gallons of water swirled around trees, pushed rocks, and filled burrows. But, as a park brochure points out, though some may see the flood as a disaster, others see it as an agent of natural change.

Perhaps the most significant change has been a reduction in the population of prairie dogs that once thrived here. Prairie dogs serve as the keystone for other species of wildlife, and without prairie dogs these other species are diminished. Burrowing owls, rattlesnakes, mountain plovers, bison, and coyotes all depend—or, as in the case of the bison, depended—on the prairie dog for various aspects of their well-being.

Naturalists have identified eighty-nine species of wildlife that are in some way associated with prairie dog colonies. Of those eighty-nine, perhaps the most interesting is the burrowing owl—a tiny, 8-inch elflike owl that nests in April and May in the cool, deserted burrows of prairie dogs. Historically seen along the Cold Desert Trail, the owls' days are numbered—their fate tied to the decline of the prairie dog. The small populations of black-footed ferrets are gone from the wild now, as their only source of food was the prairie dog. Prairie dogs once numbered in the billions but are now diminished by perhaps 90 to 95 percent.

Do enough prairie dogs still exist to rebuild to preflood populations? No one knows, but as park naturalists point out, disasters such as sudden floods make a case for maintaining wildlife populations in substantial numbers— otherwise, localized disasters might eventually eliminate a species of wildlife altogether. If you see prairie dogs on your walk, please share your sightings; they will bring much cheer to monument naturalists hoping to see a restoration of the prairie dog and all other species associated with it.

Though prairie dogs and burrowing owls may have to be considered a bonus, there are many other interesting features to be discovered during a hike on this cold-desert trail. Begin this short stroll by canvassing the surrounding area for the various types of vegetation growing here. A quick glance will show the presence of rabbitbrush, big sagebrush, cottonwood, shadscale, bud sage, and various species of grass. Rabbitbrush is plentiful because it is one of the first plants to return to a site following a disturbance. Botanists refer to such species as a "pioneer species." Pioneer plants are specific types of vegetation that sprout up following a disturbance by fire or some other agent of modification, such as a natural flood. Different species grace different climatic areas, and along this cold-desert trail rabbitbrush serves as the pioneer.

Though the trail offers an overview of recent events, it also provides for a hands-on exploration of the adaptations plants have made to survive in a cold and dry area. You're probably familiar with one of the trail's more conspicuous plants, big sagebrush, but perhaps not with its water-retention characteristics. Big sagebrush collects water by virtue of its ubiquitous root system. Spreading like the strands of a spider's web is a series of shallow roots that "suck up" almost any drop of water that falls on the ground overhead. But water in the desert is not a reliable commodity, and big sagebrush has yet another method of extracting water in a dry environment.

Big sagebrush produces a taproot that may descend as deep as 13 feet— reaching down to the water table, which generally never dries. Little wonder big sagebrush is so conspicuous. Just smell the air for that familiar pungent odor.

As well as water-extracting capabilities, big sagebrush has other techniques for retaining life-giving water, some of which it has in common with other cold-desert plants. In dry months the leaf pores close early in the morning to retain water. Other plants use this feature, too, and have adapted to maximize the production of chlorophyll during photosynthesis. When temperatures are hot, various plant species drop their large spring leaves and replace them with small summer leaves—leaves that can maximize food production while minimizing water loss. That's the way sage functions here.

Other plants employ other survival techniques. Look closely and on some you'll see tiny hairs, intended to prevent desiccation. Yet others have acquired a waxy covering to retain water during hot summer days. The list, though not endless, is certainly long.

For such a short hike, the trail packs much information. It represents an overview of but one of the monument's three life zones. Should you drive from here to Harpers Corner, other trails offering overviews of different life zones await you. They, too, should be explored.

# Nature Hike 4: Plug Hat Trail

**TYPE OF TRAIL:** A self-guided loop nature trail.

**TOTAL DISTANCE:** 0.25 mile.

**ELEVATION CHANGE:** None.

**TIME REQUIRED:** 30 to 45 minutes.

**MAPS:** *Harpers Corner Trail Guide*, available at the visitor center; National Geographic Trails Illustrated Map #220.

**DIFFICULTY:** Easy.

**STARTING POINT:** Plug Hat Trail and the picnic area are 4.3 miles from the visitor center up the Harpers Corner Scenic Drive (see map in Chapter 5, Driving Tours, page 24). Park at the picnic area on your left. To reach the drive, start at Monument Headquarters Visitor Center (Colorado), 25 miles east of Jensen, Utah, on U.S. Highway 40. The entrance is on the north side of the road, 2 miles east of Dinosaur, Colorado.

**TAKE ALONG:** Camera, binoculars.

**The hike:** First take a short stroll past the picnic tables to the rim; you'll be treated to the sights of the Colorado Plateau. Rainbow-colored rocks (derived from iron, manganese, and other elements) abound, as well as mesas and buttes. The angles of the bedrock here are interesting; they don't change overly much due to lack of rain and soil cover.

In the distance you'll see the Morrison Formation (about 148 million years old), famous for its hidden secrets—the Jurassic period fossil bones of the great *Brontosaurus*, smaller dinosaurs, mammals, and amphibians that once thrived here. (You'll need to visit the dinosaur quarry to view the bones that have been uncovered so far.)

Now cross the road and walk the easy Plug Hat Trail, where you'll be introduced to a piñon-juniper forest. From this vantage you'll also be rewarded with an all-encompassing view of the Uinta Basin.

# Nature Hike 5: Harpers Corner Trail

**TYPE OF TRAIL:** An out-and-back self-guided nature trail.

**TOTAL DISTANCE:** 2 miles.

**ELEVATION CHANGE:** 100 feet.

**TIME REQUIRED:** 1½ to 2 hours.

**MAPS:** *Harpers Corner Trail Guide,* available in visitor centers or at the trailhead; National Geographic Trails Illustrated Map #220.

**DIFFICULTY:** Moderate.

**STARTING POINT:** At the terminus of Harpers Corner Scenic Drive (see map in Chapter 5, Driving Tours, page 24). To reach the drive, start at Monument Headquarters Visitor Center
(Colorado), 25 miles east of Jensen, Utah, on U.S. Highway 40.
The entrance is on the north side of the road, 2 miles east of Dinosaur, Colorado.

**TAKE ALONG:** Sturdy shoes, water, camera, and binoculars.

**The hike:** For those who enjoy up-close and personal dramas, ones that have allowed geologists and botanists to unlock mysteries of the past, Harpers Corner may satisfy that urge. But because most won't have the geological or botanical insights of a research scientist, we won't make Harpers Corner a mystery walk. Still, as you begin your hike, you might start with a puzzle. Begin by questioning the presence of the reddish rocks along the trail. How did they get here?

The rock is a type of sandstone, and if you examine one you'll see it is composed of a fine sand that pressure has compacted into a solid piece. Despite its compact appearance, if you tapped it with a light hammer, the rock would crack apart, revealing a sandlike consistency. We geological wannabes can be fairly sure the rock seen here belongs to one of the groups described earlier in the book, which were laid down almost a billion years ago by vast inland seas.

Geologists familiar with the entire area say that they've found such sandstone not only here but also in the Uintas and along the Green River—in Whirlpool Canyon, just below. Synthesizing this information, they say that the rounded sandstone rocks originated in the Uintas and were washed here eons ago. The question, then, is how did all these rocks of congealed sand come to occupy an area 7,500 feet above sea level? Put another way, how can this sandstone be higher than its source of origin? To answer that question we must look for additional clues.

Look now at some of the other rocks along the trail, and you may see they are embedded with fossils. What you're seeing are botanical segments and the shells of creatures that lived long ago in an ancient sea. Many of these same

*Views of the Green River and cliffs from Harpers Corner Trail.*

types of creatures thrive in contemporary waters, so you might conclude that this area was once part of that long-ago sea. You are correct.

And now another question: How did that ancient sea get from down there to up here? Solve that puzzle and you'll have the sandstone answer. But unless you are steeped in historical geology, it won't be obvious. We'll have to rely on the word of scientists who have studied the earth's crust.

Conceptually, the process is simple. Millions of years ago, huge "plates" were floating (they still are, but we can't yet evaluate their futuristic effect) on a molten sea of lava when they collided. The impact wasn't sudden, as in a car crash; it was subtle, occurring over millions of years.

As the crashed plates shoved against one another, they were uplifted, creating mountains. Eventually, because of their weight the blocks tilted, perhaps a bit like Italy's Leaning Tower of Pisa. After that, other forces began to exert themselves. About midway between the Green River (to your right as you walk toward the overlook) there occurred a point of weakness. Geologists refer to such areas of weakness as faults, and this fault is known as the Mitten Park Fault. You can explore this area from other areas of the monument.

Though we have now spanned almost a billion years, our geological story is not quite finished. The dinosaurs have been gone now for almost 65 million years. To help us understand the landscape that sprawls before us, we have the past several million years. Because the final chapter is recent (from a geological perspective) and much more visible, given adequate time you could probably piece much of it together. This final chapter is the one resulting from the emergence of the Green and Yampa Rivers.

You can see the tortuous route the Yampa River has carved in its journey toward its confluence with the Green River at Echo Park to your east. As the crow flies you are about 3 miles from that point; it's where Steamboat Rock enters the water. But you can't quite see that either, for the "brow" of the "steamboat" blocks your view. Still, you can see the river's winding route, and isn't it grand? Just look at the way the canyon and river twist and turn.

And now a question. Which came first, the river or the mountains? There's no real way of telling without additional information, but if you were to guess that the rivers came first, you'd be in good company. John Wesley Powell theorized that the rivers were already flowing when the mountains began to be uplifted. What Powell could not know—and you really can't either—is that certain layers existed that were redeposited in a way that would have been impossible had the rivers already existed. The layers also provide geologists with the timing of these various occurrences. Putting it all together, geologists know the mountains were uplifted about 65 million years ago and that the rivers came much later, about five to six million years ago.

In broad geological brush strokes, that's about it. The rocks have been laid and uplifted, and in our imaginings the rivers have worked their magic. What's remaining is to clothe the valley's flanks and cap those craggy domes.

# Harpers Corner Botany

Allow your gaze and interests to wander anew. Notice the abundant vegetation. Dominating the area where you began your hike are stands of piñon pine and juniper, stunted because this lofty land is so consistently dry and windy. As a result, even though these trees may be old, they are small. But Harpers Corner Trail explains more. Near trail's end, grand vistas open up for a panorama to the west and the north. And here a different tree has emerged.

You can easily identify this new species by picking up a pinecone. Notice the numerous three-pronged bracts that cover the cone. No evergreen other than Douglas fir has bracts with three prongs.

Because Douglas fir is found in but few places in Dinosaur, and because those places are located at some considerable distance from the main and much more luxuriant stands of Douglas fir, the species' presence represents a botanical outlier—that is, a stand growing at some considerable distance from its normal range. Consequently, you might wonder how Douglas fir has managed to establish a toehold here.

Simply stated, the trees may occupy an area once surrounded by vast stands of a similar species. When conditions changed, others of its kind perished, leaving behind only this small pocket. It alone exists because it alone finds the right conditions. Here in Dinosaur this outlier requires specific and unique quantities of water; at this elevation those specific and unique quantities are found only on this particular north-facing slope.

Though these trees most likely do represent a carryover from the past, they could have gotten here another way. As a clue you might notice the presence of piñon jays, known for their love of nuts and seeds. The jays serve as vectors of dissemination. The seeds they eat often pass through the birds largely unaltered. The birds' droppings have the power to create forests.

Besides the interesting geological and botanical tales, there remains one final reason to make this hike: It offers an incredible view of Echo Park and Whirlpool Canyon. If for no other reason than to see these grand sprawls of beauty, you should make hiking Harpers Corner Trail one of your priorities.

# Nature Hike 6: Gates of Lodore Nature Trail

**TYPE OF TRAIL:** Self-guided out-and-back hike.

**TOTAL DISTANCE:** 1.5 miles.

**ELEVATION CHANGE:** 75 feet.

**TIME REQUIRED:** Approximately 1 hour.

**MAPS:** Intermountain Natural History Association pamphlet (25 cents); National Geographic Trails Illustrated Map #220.

**DIFFICULTY:** Easy; it's best to hike here in early morning or late afternoon during the hot season.

**STARTING POINT:** From Gates of Lodore Campground, about a two-and-a-half-hour drive from the dinosaur quarry. This is the north end of the monument, about 120 miles from Monument Headquarters. It is reached by taking U.S. Highway 40 east from Jensen, Utah (the town just outside the dinosaur quarry), toward Colorado, passing in 25 miles the Dinosaur National Monument Headquarters Visitor Center. Continue on US 40 for about 58 miles to the town of Maybell, Colorado. Go left at Maybell onto State Road 318, and go approximately 37 miles, until you come to a left turn onto the hard-packed County Road 34. There is a sign here indicating that this is the road to Gates of Lodore. Follow CR 34 for about 9 miles—it leads directly into the campground. The trail begins at the south end of Gates of Lodore Campground.

**The hike:** This short, easy hike takes you above the Green River, which is flowing somewhat placidly here out of the Browns Park area. You can walk to the beginning of the Canyon of Lodore, where river runners are abruptly thrust into the riffles and rapids of this incredibly beautiful, rugged area.

The hike is intended to introduce visitors to the red cliffs of the canyon and the flora and fauna of the area. You'll see an abundance of cheatgrass here, a nonnative invasive grass that most animals cannot eat. Lichen cover the rocks. Since lichen are sensitive to air pollution, the brighter the colors the cleaner the air. So far, pollution evidently hasn't taken hold here. Another amazing phenomenon is that you are actually standing on the Uinta Mountain Group, which comprises some of the oldest rocks in the monument. Because the geology here is complex but fascinating, we suggest purchasing a book or pamphlet on Dinosaur's rocks. The Green River cut right across the mountains here and carved out the Canyon of Lodore.

Utah juniper trees grow here as well as some piñon pine. Plants such as black greasewood, saltbush, and sagebrush also do well. You won't find much

Gates of Lodore Nature Trail

cacti; this is a cold-desert environment, and cacti can't survive through the harsh winters. But there are some that bloom in spring, brightening the landscape.

Bighorn sheep were ancient dwellers in the area, as attested to by the many 1,000-year-old petroglyphs. But the sheep you might glimpse today are from a group introduced in the 1950s—the native bighorn sheep disappeared in the 1940s.

John Wesley Powell (who boated the entire Green River in 1869 and 1871) wrote while camped at Lodore that now he and his men were entering "the great unknown." One of his crew is credited with naming the canyon after an English poem by Robert Southey titled "The Cataract of Lodore."

The Gates of Lodore is a quiet area, a place of beauty and much history, and is well worth exploring.

# Nature Hike 7: Geology Trail

**TYPE OF TRAIL:** A three-quarter loop (you begin at Douglass Dinosaur Quarry and end up at the shuttle bus parking lot).

**TOTAL DISTANCE:** 0.75 to 1 mile.

**ELEVATION CHANGE:** Slight.

**TIME REQUIRED:** 1 hour.

**MAPS:** None; this is a ranger-led hike.

**DIFFICULTY:** Easy.

**STARTING POINT:** Douglass Dinosaur Quarry (see map in this chapter, page 46).

**The hike:** Because this hike is mostly downhill, it is an easy hike. We say *mostly* downhill, but there are places involving a bit of rock scrambling if the ranger leading the hike that day wishes to point out some still-imbedded dinosaur bones. For most the hike would be meaningless unless you joined one of the scheduled interpretive walks with a park ranger. In fact, in the interest of pre-serving Dinosaur's fossils, the park discourages individuals from striking out alone. But make this hike you should, for the short hike descends through six geological formations—meaning that when you reach the bottom, you will have hiked through eighty million years of time.

Dinosaur National Monument has the most complete geological record of any U.S. national park. As a keeper of earth's march of time as it is revealed in rock, the record exceeds even that of the Grand Canyon.

The hike begins in the Morrison Formation, the layer in which dinosaur bones are most commonly located. A dozen or more feet farther, the Morrison Formation gives way to the Stump Formation, rock you can see outside the quarry and which is characterized by a crumbling appearance. The formation is a repository of gastropods and other marine organisms. It is also the area in which our ranger/naturalist guide showed us petrified wood. When you realize these fossils existed during the time dinosaurs roamed the area, you understand what an incredible sight you are seeing. Also present in the Morrison Forma-tion was chert, a dark rock used by Indians for making arrowheads.

About halfway through the hike, our guide stopped at another outcropping of the Morrison Formation and showed us a series of dinosaur bones. Examples included vertebrae and segments of a femur as well as a number of dinosaur bone chips. More than 80 percent of the bones found in Dinosaur National Monument belong to a grouping known as sauropods. The quarry has pro-duced both the greatest variety of dinosaur species and the largest number of individuals taken from any North American Jurassic period site thus far.

Farther down the trail we passed through the Cedar Mountain Formation, another formation in which dinosaur bones have been found in the monument. As we descended the trail, we also passed through the Dakota Sandstone, Mowry Shale, and Frontier Sandstone Formations. We concluded our walk near a series of petroglyphs and with a discussion of why one should not vandalize these works of art.

A short walk from the petroglyphs returns you to the parking lot.

# Chapter 8
# Hiking Trails

## Hiking Trail 1: Green River Campground to Split Mountain Campground

Take a 1.8-mile (one-way) walk along a path above the Green River between Green River Campground and the southern end of Split Mountain Campground. The trail departs from the northernmost end of Green River Campground and meanders along the base of the hills rising from the Green River. It's a scenic, fun, fairly easy walk that offers spectacular views of Split Mountain and the river. In early morning and late afternoon, the colors on the mountains are beautiful, generally offering superb photo opportunities. Cacti sometimes bloom here, which can be a treat, as cacti aren't plentiful in the high desert of Dinosaur.

To access this path, turn into Green River Campground off Cub Creek Road about 1.5 miles past the turnoff to Split Mountain. Drive down the hill

### Green River Campground to Split Mountain Campground

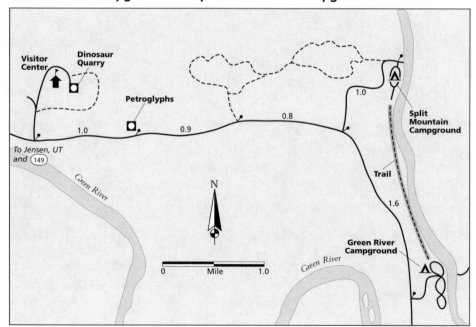

to the campsites, taking a left turn at the ranger station to access the Loop A circle of sites. Go halfway around the circle; you will see the sign for the path on your right.

As an alternative you can walk north to south by driving into Split Mountain Campground, parking in the lot, walking to the most southern end of the campsites, and accessing the path from there into Green River Campground.

# Hiking Trails 2 and 3: Hog Canyon and Box Canyon Trails

**TYPE OF TRAIL:** Out and back.

**TOTAL DISTANCE:** 1.5 miles total for Hog Canyon; approximately 0.75 mile total for Box Canyon.

**ELEVATION CHANGE:** None.

**TIME REQUIRED:** 1 to 2 hours.

**MAPS:** Intermountain Natural History Association booklet (50 cents); National Geographic Trails Illustrated Map #220.

**DIFFICULTY:** Easy.

**STARTING POINT:** Hog Canyon begins at the terminus of the Tour of the Tilted Rocks Driving Tour at the Josie Morris Cabin area. To reach the Hog Canyon trailhead, enter the monument through the western (Utah) entrance at the dinosaur quarry. The trail leaves from the path between Josie's Cabin and the spring. Box Canyon is accessed at the north end of the circular parking lot.

**The hikes:** Hog Canyon Trail provides one of the park's most delightful short hikes, passing through several habitat types, including a canyon of high cliffs that offers a delightful reprieve from summer heat. The trail begins to the east of the Josie Morris Cabin near a small spring. Adjacent to the spring the park provides several signs that interpret the significance of water to Josie and to others in the West. Josie fought for her water rights and eventually constructed a series of small dams intended to trap the water so necessary for her cattle.

About 50 feet east of the spring, the trail crosses the creek. A sign addresses the significance of natural sounds and their blend with the hogs Josie maintained as a source of her livelihood. On the day we hiked the trail, the sounds of birds overwhelmed all else. Yet a few feet farther along the trail, another interpretive sign explained the method Josie used in Hog Canyon to restrain her animals. Hog Canyon prevented the egress of livestock from three sides, and a rail fence prevented their egress from the fourth.

The trail also passes through an area where a rare orchid was discovered in 1989. Discovery of the *Spiranthes diluvialis* lured a number of conservationists to the area, all interested in preserving the species. In a rhetorical manner, the monument questions why so many might seek to preserve one small plant. Though there are many answers, certainly one is that scientists may find the cure for some rare disease, just as botanists have discovered molds that are important as antibiotics and willow as the source for aspirin. Aesthetically, of course, the plant adds "diversity and stability," as the monument so eloquently states.

# Hog Canyon and Box Canyon Trails

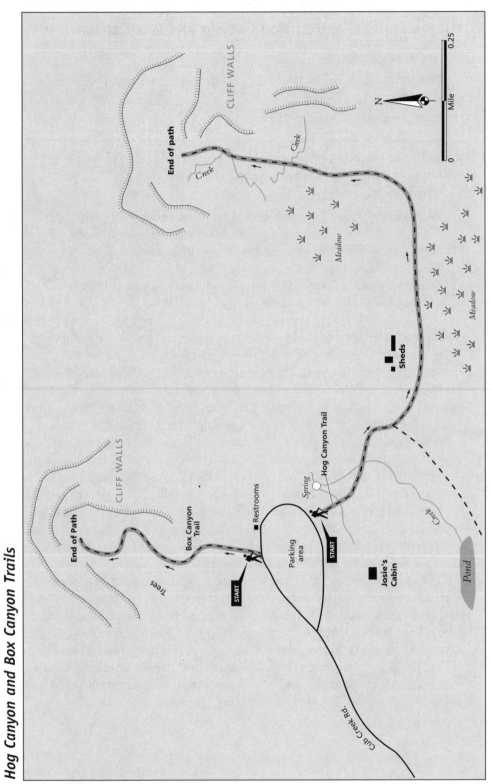

The trail then proceeds through a glen of boxelder and cottonwood to break into an open meadow. On the day of our June hike, the trail was carpeted with several acres of the gorgeous bee plant. We saw a profusion of other plants as well, including mint, sage, wild rose, and yarrow (a plant characterized by numerous small white flowers crowning its stem). Though extracts of yarrow are used to stimulate the heart, if eaten wild the plant can produce just the opposite effect. It produces a toxin that in sufficient quantities can stop the heart.

About 0.5 mile later, the trail enters Hog Canyon, a place once used by the ancient Fremont people and more recently by Josie Morris. When we entered the canyon, it was cool, and the sounds of wrens and flickers filled the morning air. Nearby, a small stream covered with watercress coursed through the canyon. We followed the creek, which paralleled the trail to a point along the west wall, to where it emerged from beneath rock running along the base of the cliff. The water was clear and inviting but unsafe to drink.

At this point, the canyon walls rise abruptly. The walls represent deposits laid down in the Paleozoic era, when coastal sand dunes claimed the area. Typically, the rocks are a light tan; here in Hog Canyon they are streaked with the black deposits of manganese. Often such walls were used by the Fremont for inscribing petroglyphs and pictographs, but no such art exists in Hog Canyon.

About 0.75 mile from Josie's Cabin, the trail terminates at the now-narrowing walls. The coolness here on a hot day is a welcome respite. The National Park Service requests that hikers not climb up the cliffs or walls at trail's end, because they are steep and slippery with sudden drop-offs. From here we retraced our steps and enjoyed once again the natural sights and sounds of Hog Canyon.

On hot days Box Canyon offers a pleasant short stroll to the end of the second of Josie Morris's canyons. It was another place where she was able to corral her livestock with natural fences on three sides. There are no interpretive signs along this sandy wash of a trail, but it's a fun, shady hike to the end where the canyon walls rise steeply in front of you. We felt that Josie probably used the Hog Canyon meadows and canyon more than she used Box Canyon.

*Hog Canyon Trail at the Josie Morris homestead.*

# Hiking Trail 4: Jones Hole Trail and Jones Hole National Fish Hatchery

**TYPE OF TRAIL:** Out and back.

**TYPE OF TRIP:** A full day. You are permitted to camp at Ely Creek Campground, provided there is room and you possess a backcountry permit from the Douglass Dinosaur Quarry or Headquarters Visitor Center.

**TOTAL DISTANCE:** 8 miles of trail, out and back, plus side trips, if desired.

**ELEVATION CHANGE:** 200 feet

**TIME REQUIRED:** 4 hours minimum, usually longer, to hike, plus a 2- to 3-hour round-trip drive from the monument.

**MAPS:** Intermountain Natural History Association pamphlet; Dinosaur National Monument free handout map; National Geographic Trails Illustrated Map #220.

**DIFFICULTY:** Easy.

**STARTING POINT:** Jones Hole National Fish Hatchery.

**THE TRAILHEAD:** Getting to the trailhead involves some driving (47 miles one-way from the quarry), but don't despair—the scenery en route to Jones Hole National Fish Hatchery is spectacular. The road winds up Diamond Mountain, which offers beautiful views and passes scattered ranches with acres and acres of sagebrush fields.

Exit Dinosaur National Monument from the entrance station on Utah Highway 149 going toward Jensen. In 4 miles you will cross Brush Creek. Take the first right turn after the creek onto Brush Creek Road. Go approximately 5 miles to a right-hand turn onto a good dirt road, following the sign to Island Park Road. Go 4 miles; do *not* take the right turn to Island Park, but continue straight on the dirt road for another 2 miles. Once you get on the paved road, stay on that road for 33 more miles to Jones Hole National Fish Hatchery, where the road ends. The trail begins at the south end of the hatchery at the last outdoor fish-holding tank.

From Vernal, Utah, follow these directions: Go east from Vernal on 500 North, off Vernal Avenue. At Mile 2.9 go left at a junction. At Mile 7.8 continue straight at the next junction. (The road to the right goes to Island Park and Rainbow Park in Dinosaur National Monument.) Go 2.2 miles to Brush Creek Junction; stay straight for 8.3 more miles. You are now on the top of Diamond Mountain Plateau. At this junction, take the left-hand road and go 4 miles to Diamond Gulch Junction; continue straight for 3.2 miles to another junction. Continue straight on the paved road for 5.5 miles to the junction with

Jones Hole Area

START

Deluge Shelter Petroglyphs
Jones Hole Trail

WHIRLPOOL CANYON

Jones Hole Creek

Harper's Corner Scenic Drive

UTAH COLORADO

Jones Hole Fish Hatchery

Ely Creek

Island Park Trail

Ruple Ranch

Island Park

Rainbow Park

McKee Springs

Petroglyphs

1.0

5.4

PLEASE NOTE: The Island/Rainbow Park Road crosses clay soils that become IMPASSABLE WHEN WET. When dry, the road may be driven with care in most passenger cars.

DIAMOND MOUNTAIN

14

17

Jones Hole Rd.

To Browns Park via Crouse Canyon (rough road)

Green River

Island Park Rd.

12.0

Dinosaur Quarry

Area of Cub Creek Petroglyphs

To Elk Springs, CO

40

149

N

Miles

0        4.0

Water tank

2.0

Triangle bridge

4.1

Brush Creek

4.8

Brush Creek Rd. (rough)

3.5

6

County dump

4.0

3

Jensen

40

To Flaming Gorge

44

191

Vernal

Pot Creek. Stay on the paved road here and go another 9 miles to Jones Hole National Fish Hatchery.

**The history of the area:** Diamond Mountain Plateau is nearly 8,000 feet in elevation. It was named for the exploits of two "inventive" men, P. Arnold and J. Slack. These two were apparently able to convince bankers in California that they had discovered a field of diamonds on a mountain in Utah. Unbeknownst to the bankers, the men had bought real diamonds and scattered them there, and the rush was on to form a huge corporation. The two men quickly sold their shares, made a lot of money, and disappeared just as quickly. It wasn't long before the diamond field was revealed as a fake. Mr. Arnold was caught, but his partner never was.

Diamond Mountain Plateau consists of some private farmland (mostly winter wheat) and some Bureau of Land Management land. The area also provides good elk and deer hunting. According to history, cattle rustlers often hid their stolen beef up here. In general the area served as a hideaway for outlaws of all stripes.

Visitors are welcome to tour the fish hatchery. Brook, brown, cutthroat, and rainbow trout are all raised here for the waters of Utah, Colorado, and Wyoming. The hatching pools are indoors; the outdoor ponds contain trout in various stages of development.

**The hike:** Though John Wesley Powell named this splendid area of geology, Indian art, and superb fishing in 1871 for his expedition's talented topographer, most believe the name did not take hold until Charley Jones hid in the area after shooting a man. Charley believed he had killed the man, but following a year of hiding, when he learned the man had lived, Jones is said to have declared, "You mean I can finally get out of this hole?" The name took hold.

Jones Hole Trail begins at the hatchery, at the end of the fish tanks. A lovely narrow path meandering along bubbling, clear Jones Hole Creek, which comes from an underground source, offers lots of shade in the form of box elder trees. Sage, juniper, and skunk-bush sumac also line the trail. The narrow, sandy path is rocky, so wear sturdy boots, carry lots of water, and take a hat, sunscreen, and bug repellant. Creek water should not be drunk without proper purification.

You begin your hike at an elevation of 5,000 feet, but the elevation changes throughout the hike are only about 200 feet. After 1.5 miles cross Jones Hole Creek on a small wood bridge. Soon you'll see the first sign of rock art on the right. The Fremont people made these pictographs almost 1,000 years ago, and they are faint. Walk but a short distance farther and you come to Deluge Shelter. This area was excavated in the mid-1960s. A flash flood crashed through the canyon in 1966, destroying the archaeologists' camp but leaving the rock art intact—thus the name.

*Pictographs at Deluge Shelter.*

The pictographs at Deluge Shelter are beautiful, and many are well preserved. You'll see bighorn sheep, spirals, and other forms. Many hours have been spent analyzing their meaning, but in the final analysis they are just theories. Your theory may be just as meaningful as those provided by archaeologists. There are several good books on the market offering suggestions for rock art interpretation.

Some things are known, however. Archaeologists have been able to determine from their finds that the shelter area probably was used for some 7,000 years by the Great Basin, the Uncompahgre Plateau, and the Northwestern Plains cultures. Few places like this exist. Furthermore, researchers were able to trace the progression of sophistication of these peoples from use of the spear to the atlatl to the bow and arrow. Occupancy of Deluge Shelter was between 5000 B.C. and A.D. 1850.

To make the pictographs found here, the Fremont people would grind iron oxide from the sandstone and then mix it with plant or animal oil to make a resilient orange color. Unfortunately, inconsiderate visitors have also been at work in Deluge, adding their names to the panels. In some cases they have actually taken potshots at the art with rifles. By so doing they have become thieves of time.

Continuing past Deluge Shelter, a five-minute walk down the trail takes you to a junction. You have now come 2.2 miles. A turn to the right here would take you on Island Park Trail, 8 miles one-way, and you would end up at the historic Ruple Ranch in Island Park. Another option is to take the right-hand fork for only 0.5 mile to the Ely Creek waterfall, a good cooling-off spot.

If you wish to keep your original hike plans, turn left at the junction, step across tiny Ely Creek, and you're in Ely Creek Campground. Ely has two campsites, though you'll need a permit to stay. Many who do stay usually come for the superb fishing. As one hiker said, "What better place to fish than below a hatchery?"

From this point it is another 1.8 miles to the Whirlpool Canyon section of the Green River and the ranger station. For some, Ely Creek is a good turn-around point, making your total hike 4 miles instead of 8.

If you do hike to the river, you'll see that the area has a number of camp-sites. These are reserved for those who are running the river. Hikers are asked to respect the privacy of those camped here.

The Jones Hole area offers superb angling as well as a multitude of other features. Wildlife of various forms, including bighorn sheep, are abundant in the area. There is also an abundance of bird life, numerous wildflowers, and a range of geological formations that span more than 600 million years. At 600 million years, the Lodore Formation is the oldest; at 310 million years, the Weber Formation is the youngest. Sandwiched between are Humbug, Madison Limestone, and Morgan Sandstone Formations, which together offer a verita-ble palette of artist's colors.

We made this hike on a lovely, cool mid-June weekend and met a few fly fishermen and only a few hikers—in other words, no crowds. *NOTE:* If you wish to fish here, you must have a Utah fishing license; flies and artificial lures only are to be used (no live bait).

## Hiking
### Outlaw Trail

Embark on an 18- to 20-mile rugged backpack adventure on the old Outlaw Trail, which could take you from the northern banks of the Yampa River, where it enters the Green River by Jenny Lind Rock, all the way to Lodore Campground. For this longer hike, see National Geographic Trails Illustrated Map #220 (Dinosaur National Monument). You'll need to register with the park for a backcountry permit—you'll probably want to spend three to four nights camping. Also talk with rangers and get their advice as to additional topo maps and the most advantageous way to find routes.

When we visited Dinosaur National Monument, we met a group of young people from the Outward Bound School. They had rafted down the Yampa River and were camping for the night in Echo Park. From there they planned to backtrack slightly, crossing the Yampa River (probably someone would ferry them by raft) at the confluence with the Green River, climb a bluff, and follow the Outlaw Trail for about three days to Gates of Lodore. What an enviable adventure!

### Island Park Trail

Backcountry hike Island Park Trail (off Ely Creek) at Jones Hole. When you visit the Jones Hole National Fish Hatchery, you can walk down Jones Hole Trail for 1.8 miles to the junction with Island Park Trail, which turns to the right at the trail sign. In 0.5 mile you'll come to Ely Creek Falls. Go another 0.3 mile to a fork in the trail, and turn left. It is 7.5 miles from here to the end of the trail at Ruple Ranch in Island Park. The trail climbs out of Jones Hole and crosses Red Wash at about the halfway mark. Obviously, this hike involves a shuttle, unless you plan to backtrack to Jones Hole. Check with rangers about trail conditions, maps, and backcountry permits. *HINT:* Take time to explore for Indian artifacts.

### Ruple Point Trail

This 4-mile (one-way) hike departs from Harpers Corner Road about 1 mile north of the turnoff to Echo Park Road. The trailhead is on the left as you proceed north. The hike traverses Ruple Ridge, which at its terminus offers a

# Island Park Trail and Surrounding Area

PLEASE NOTE: The Island/Rainbow Park Road crosses clay soils that become IMPASSABLE WHEN WET. When dry, the road may be driven with care in most passenger cars.

N

Miles

0        4.0

To Browns Park via
Crouse Canyon
(rough road)

DIAMOND MOUNTAIN

Jones Hole Rd.

14

17

Jones Hole Trail

START

Deluge Shelter Petroglyphs

Jones Hole Fish Hatchery

Ely Creek

Jones Hole Creek

Island Park Trail

Ruple Ranch

Island Park

5.4

Rainbow Park

1.0

McKee Springs

Petroglyphs

WHIRLPOOL CANYON

Harpers Corner Scenic Drive

COLORADO

UTAH

Green River

Island Park Rd.

12.0

Area of Cub Creek Petroglyphs

Dinosaur Quarry

3.5

149

Jensen

40

To Elk Springs, CO

Water tank

Triangle bridge

2.0

4.1

Brush Creek

4.8

6

4.0

Brush Creek Rd. (rough)

3

County dump

191

44

Vernal

40

To Flaming Gorge

## Ruple Point Trail

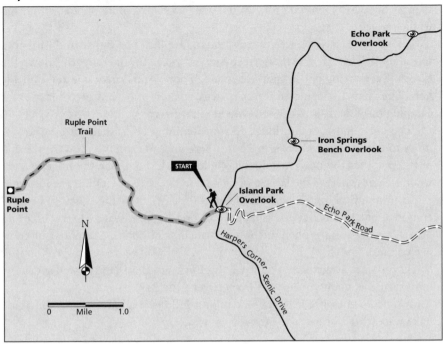

panoramic view of Split Mountain, Rainbow Park, the Green River, and lands beyond. Check with rangers about trail conditions and maps.

## Driving and Walking
### Island/Rainbow Park Road

Island/Rainbow Park Road (see Island Park Trail map) leads to McKee Spring petroglyphs, Rainbow Park, Island Park, Ruple Ranch, and the petrified sand dunes. Check with rangers or with park personnel at the visitor centers about road conditions, and keep an eye on the weather forecasts yourself. Following rain, this road may be impassable. From the dinosaur quarry to road's end (at Island Park), the trip is about 31.5 miles one-way (see Island Park Trail map). There are no services on this road. Rainbow Park Campground has two sites and a pit toilet, but no water.

This exploration on a not-crowded, good dirt road offers much for the Dinosaur National Monument visitor. The first stop along the way is the McKee Spring petroglyph site, which is explained in more detail in Chapter 4 (Dinosaur National Monument, page 13). For most of the drive you have been outside park boundaries; McKee Spring is on the left immediately after you reenter the park. Here you can stretch your legs, take some photos, and listen to the silence.

About 1 mile past McKee Spring, the road splits. The right-hand turn goes to Rainbow Park. Here's where river runners put in for one-day trips down the Green River, taking out at Split Mountain. There is no drinking water available here, but there are picnic tables, fireplaces, a vault toilet, and two tent sites for camping (no fee). It is a pleasant stop along the way.

The left-hand turn continues east on Rainbow Park Road for another 5.4 miles to Island Park. There is no water here and no camping. Toward the end of the road lies the now-abandoned Ruple Ranch. Some say the huge cotton-wood tree near here is the largest of its kind in the state of Utah. It is enormous.

Continue back on the dirt road (heading east) from the ranch. The road ends in about 1 mile, but you can take a several-hundred-yard easterly hike and discover a fascinating phenomenon: petrified sand dunes, composed of compacted sand.

As you gaze at the river, you'll see Big Buck and Big Island as well as several others. At this point you are at Green River Mile 214.

You could spend at least half a day or a full day exploring along this road. Take water, food, sturdy shoes, and a camera.

## Running the River on Your Own

If you want to run either Green or Yampa River on your own, you must list on your permit application those Class III rivers you have already run. For the safety of your limbs—and possibly even your life—you should answer these questions honestly.

Class III rivers are categorized as those that have rocks, eddies, and rapids that are usually clear but are so narrow they require expertise in maneuvering. Rapids in this category mandate scouting. The Green and Yampa consistently offer such features, but at times they can also offer powerful and irregular waves interspersed with dangerous rocks—raising the rating to an even more dangerous category. Under such conditions, most rate Dinosaur's rapids as a "good solid III." In reality, under those circumstances the Yampa and the Green may sometimes flirt with a rating of IV. Class V rapids are considered impassable.

Essentially, the difficulty of running the Green and Yampa depends on the season of the year and on the amount of water the Bureau of Reclamation is releasing from Flaming Gorge Reservoir into the Green. Unfortunately, water releases can often be unpredictable. When releases are high on the Green—perhaps 6,000 cubic feet per second (cfs) or higher—rapids such as Upper and Lower Disaster and Hell's Half Mile (all above Echo Park) could almost be designated as Class IV rapids.

In an attempt to clarify this sometimes vague rating, we offer the following comparisons: the Grand Canyon of the Colorado (which sometimes approaches Class V), Idaho's Middle Fork of the Salmon (IV), and Montana's Middle Fork of the Flathead (III). Of course there are many others.

## Fees and Shuttle Service

After much deliberation, if you conclude that you can safely navigate Dinosaur's rivers, by all means apply for a $15 permit. Additionally, you'll be required to pay a registration fee of $185 for multiday use or $20 for a single day. Because each private party can include about twenty people, the larger the party the cheaper the per-person rate. If your party consists of only two people (as in our case), then you are paying a premium price.

If you are traveling by yourself and have but one vehicle, you will need to hire someone to shuttle your vehicle. We used Wilkins Bus Transportation and eventually paid about $90 for that service. Because no one else was scheduled for shuttle service with them on the day we needed our vehicle, initially Mr. Wilkins asked $150. What a nice surprise to find a refund of $60, along with a note explaining that another party had needed their vehicle shuttled, hence the refund. In this age and time such honesty is heartwarming.

## What You Need

In addition to the fees and shuttle service (we've listed other shuttle services in Appendix C), if you are running the river in your own private party—or by yourself—you must satisfy the requirements of the park's equipment list. This list can be viewed on the Internet or sent to you from the Dinosaur Monument River Office. Essentially the list is straightforward, though there are several items that should be discussed.

First, life preservers or flotation devices must meet U.S. Coast Guard requirements. That means they must be more than an inexpensive fishing or water-skiing vest, and they cannot be of the "horse collar" type—which looks like the halter for a draft horse. The requirements state ". . . either Type I, Type III whitewater/canoeing/kayak or Type V must be worn by each participant while on the river. . . . Type III and Type V life jackets must be approved for whitewater activities." If these designations confuse you, look at the flotation devices sold by Cascade Outfitters (see their Web site listed in Appendix F). Because we've always floated rivers that don't require permits or mandate a check-in (ones in Montana and in Alaska), at first the designations confused us. We learned, however,  that our locally purchased vests did indeed satisfy the scrutiny of the monument's river ranger, who checks in both you and your equipment.

If you are floating on your own and want to build a fire for cooking or for warmth, you will also need to purchase a fire pan—a good one might cost several hundred dollars. Though the park lists fire pans in their equipment checklist, you won't need one if you carry a backpack stove and don't build a fire. Nor will you need a cooler if you carry freeze-dried food. You will, however, need the mandated strainer in your possession for straining waste food before washing. We never used ours because we ate everything we cooked. But you never know.

One piece of equipment not listed in the monument's suggested checklist is an inexpensive, ingenious device known as Oars-Up, available from Cascade Outfitters for about $6.95. Oars-Up consists of three rings welded together that conform to the diameter of the oars used by serious boatmen. When ashore, you slip your two oars plus your mandatory spare oar into Oars-Up. Then you wrap a tarp around your now-standing tripod and bungi the tarp to the three standing oars, using the grommets in the tarp as points of attachment. If others are nearby, Oars-Up erected with the tarp provides a degree of privacy.

Portable toilet requirements are a major consideration because of the cost and the needs they must fill. First and foremost they must be self-contained and capable of holding all contents, even if you should flip and the container be pounded against rocks. We used a commercial RV porta-potty, which contains waste with a sliding valve. Though ours met the minimum requirements, in the future we may consider purchasing what old-time rafters affectionately refer to as the "Groover."

The Groover was given its name by those who first pioneered it. The first Groovers were nothing more than military surplus ammo boxes, readied by simply unsnapping the watertight clamp used to secure and protect ammunition from rain and weather. As you can imagine, sitting on the open metal box left distinct grooves on the posterior portion of one's anatomy—hence the term. Though ammo cans secured the contents when the lid was snapped in place, obviously improvements could be made. And made they have been.

If you plan to raft rivers in the Southwest, we believe this item should top your must-have list. Groovers now come with disposable plastic sacks and beautifully fitted seats, all of which runs about $300. But with one you have comfort, sanitation, and the knowledge that should you flip, and should your Groover strike a rock, the contents will not despoil the Green, Yampa, or any other river you might care to run. Plastic RV containers, though sturdy, probably can't sustain the battering from powerful waters and from hard, repeated use.

Because we take such trips as much to learn about the history and what makes the country so beautiful, we recommend a certain amount of reading material, a pillow under your head (easy in a raft), and a reliable battery headlamp, available from most sporting goods stores.

For reading material, we strongly recommend several books and pamphlets, including *The Exploration of the Colorado River and Its Canyons* by John Wesley Powell. Though the book provides a narration of all of Powell's explorations, it also provides detailed information about the Green River as it existed in 1869, before the construction of the dam at Flaming Gorge in 1963. Chapter 6, The Canyon of Lodore, and Chapter 7, From Echo Park to the Mouth of the Uinta, are must reading around nightly campfires or while holed up in your tent waiting out an evening thunderstorm. You might also want to read *Echo Park: A River Runner's Guide to the Geology.*

## Running the River with a Company

If you are one of the many who have not mastered the skills necessary to run the Green or Yampa on your own, joining a professional river-running company is a fun-filled alternative. Even if you have the skills adequate to run the Green, such an option may still be beneficial. Although our skills are acceptable, we joined Hatch Expeditions. Through them we quadrupled our river-running knowledge.

Part of this knowledge was acquired because our guides were so experienced. Our group included five rafts, all manned by professional oarsmen. Our guide had done her homework and could inform not only on the history of river running in Dinosaur, but also on the monument's geology.

Among the guides in our group was Josh Lowry, one of the world's most respected kayakers. Josh, we learned, had kayaked not only the much-respected Bio Bio in Chile, but also that country's Futalafu, which contains waterfalls that drop up to 50 feet. In his river-runner's picture portfolio, a number of prints document him and his kayak plummeting in breathtaking feats of balance and coordination—and possibly even luck.

Josh's presence documented that he had successfully run those falls, and we were awed. Obviously the man knew how to navigate rivers, and by discussing techniques for running the Yampa, we had a master tutor. How we wished we could have joined him on the Yampa before we had run the Green. Oh, well— we did survive, but more about that later.

Other guides in the group also brought areas of expertise. One was a man skilled in river rescue as well as a former chef, so you can be sure our meals satisfied the epicureans among us.

For those who would like to explore Dinosaur with a guide, we've included a list in Appendix C of those offering guide services. Prices vary, as does the type of service. All guides are endorsed by Dinosaur National Monument, but you should still check out several before settling on one. Undoubtedly they, too, come with experts and specialists that will make your trip a never-to-be-forgotten experience.

And now for some specifics on the monument's two rivers.

# The Green River

*All about me are interesting geological records. The book is open,*
*and I can read as I run. . . . The scenery was on a grand scale,*
*and never before did I live in such ecstasy for an entire month.*
—John Wesley Powell, 1869
(writing about his journey down the Green)

**GENERAL:** The Green River threads its way for 44 miles through the monument. It can be floated by joining a private concession or independently by obtaining a permit.

**PERMITS:** About 300 lottery-acquired permits are available through the River Office. Call (970) 374–2468.

**FEATURES:** Sheer canyon walls, bighorn sheep, fishing, photography, challenging rapids.

**ACCESS:** Gates of Lodore (four- to five-day trips), Echo Park (one- to two-day trips), and Rainbow Park (one-day trip). Before heading to the Green River from Dinosaur National Monument, you would do well to purchase a 1:100,000 scale map of Colorado, the Canyon of Lodore (put out by the Bureau of Land Management and sold in both Dinosaur visitor centers), and possibly Utah and Colorado state maps to help you find your way. Access the Green from the Canyon of Lodore for a multiday trip. Plan on spending the night and launching early the next morning. Include time for a hike on Gates of Lodore Nature Trail, which overlooks the canyon.

**TIME PERMITTED:** Four-day permits are most typical and facilitate the acquisition of your campsite of choice. You can apply for a longer trip (five days instead of four, with an additional fee of $35), but this is not always possible during high-use season.

**CAMPSITES:** Fourteen campsites exist along the way and are assigned by the River Office when your permit is issued. Though you may state your preference, there is no assurance you will get it, even if you've requested a trip of four days or shorter. Because Jones Hole Campsite offers hiking to petroglyphs and offers good fishing opportunities, this site is a popular one. But if that is one of your preferences, don't be dismayed if it has already been taken; other sites can be just as attractive and certainly less busy. We found each one assigned to us to be quite nice and totally clean (zero impact!).

# Green River Overview

N

Miles

0    10.0

SPLIT MOUNTAIN CANYON

Dinosaur Quarry

Green River

200

Rainbow Park

Island Park

SPLIT MOUNTAIN

210

Jones Hole

UTAH COLORADO

WHIRLPOOL CANYON

220

Echo Park

230

Green River

CANYON OF LODORE

240

Yampa River

243 ¹/₂

Lodore Ranger Station

Gates of Lodore

## Overview: The Enduring Green

The 730-mile-long Green River originates at Stroud Glacier, high on the west side of the Wind River Mountains of Wyoming among glacial lakes and mountain cascades. The 44 miles running through Dinosaur National Monument begin as the river flows out of Browns Park into Lodore and runs through the Uinta Mountains (which run east-west). When you launch your boat, you will be in water that was once snowmelt and that originated in the Wind River Range. You'll also be drifting through land that was home to tribes of the Shoshone Indians. As John Wesley Powell wrote, "It is a great hunting and fishing region, and the vigorous Shoshones still obtain a part of their livelihood from mesa and plain, river and lake."

Though Powell was the first to officially explore the Green, others preceded him. In the spring of 1825, William H. Ashley camped beside the river, determined to find new lands from which to trap beaver. In those days, most referred to the Green as the *Seeds-ke-dee*, a Shoshone word meaning "prairie chicken." Here Ashley shot buffalo and from the hides fashioned the first boat to run the Green—the much-used bull boat.

In looks, bull boats resemble a grapefruit cut in half with its succulence removed. To build these boats, men cut branches and fashioned them into ribs for rigidity. As you can imagine, such vessels were wobbly even on calm lake waters. It's little wonder most believe that some members of the Ashley party drowned along the turbulent Green.

Though Ashley and a few others had floated the Green before Powell, the one-armed Civil War major was the first to officially travel the river for scientific purposes. Though largely self-taught, Powell was an astute scientific observer who understood what he saw and encountered.

Some believed Powell would find waterfalls, but according to one park naturalist, Powell was more optimistic. Powell believed the silt-laden, fast-flowing Green would scour the river's bottom to such an extent that there would be no major drops. "Powell," said the naturalist, "knew water could be violent, but that it would be the annual deposit of overhead rocks that would stir things up."

Fortunately for those of us who now follow, Powell was correct in his assessment of the Green's relative wildness. Rest assured, there are no major drops. Powell also understood geology, particularly the geology through which he passed. In part based on his insights, we know that when a rafter completes the float from Lodore to the most distant takeout at Split Mountain, he or she will have passed through more than one billion years of time.

The story of geology along the Green has a number of fundamental components. Once the area was inundated repeatedly by vast inland seas. Each time the seas encroached, they deposited sediments. With time, forces beneath the earth's crust became unstable. Huge tectonic plates collided and buckled, forc-

*The Green River, just below its confluence with the Yampa River.*

ing the land upward, creating the mountains we know as the Uintas. More to the point, they created the geological features that you as a river runner may well encounter. The question is, how will you contend with those challenges? Will you succumb to the nag of fear as we did at times, or will you encounter with equanimity standing waves, sinkholes large enough to gobble a raft whole? More than likely, you'll do as we did, developing confidence as the trip progresses. But for us, it took time.

## Running the Green

Before pushing off for our four-day trip down the Green, we visited the monument's river ranger, who told us a story we really didn't want to hear. The ranger told us about a man whose raft had been flipped by brutal waters. Subsequently waves shoved him against a rock. He then had the misfortune to be trailed by his raft, which pinned him tight against the rocks. That might not have been so bad had he been someplace other than the Green, but it was a season of high water flow, and the tons of water that accompanied the man and the raft held him fast. Though the man was strong, he could not extricate himself. Fortunately, the river ranger drifted onto the scene just in the nick of time. Leaping from his raft, he swam to the man and cut him free with the knife he carried in a sheath built into his life preserver.

Additional stories were told by campers about to embark on a float. Everyone, it seemed, wanted to dramatize the experiences they'd either enjoyed previously or had shared with others. When someone told us about a commercial river guide who had lost his life on the Yampa, we wondered if we might not be literally in over our heads.

Still, we decided to set out on our own.

Although no two groups of floaters can ever duplicate an experience, we've included highlights of ours, as examples of what you might encounter.

## Overcoming Abject Fear

Eight miles after we had pushed our raft from the head of the Canyon of Lodore, we heard ahead a resounding roar. At first it was muted, but as we drifted farther, the noise intensified.

The sound was caused by the churn and pound of water on the same section of the river that had wiped out one of John Wesley Powell's four wooden boats during his exploration of the Colorado River Basin in 1869. As we approached the source of the noise, we began trying to reassure ourselves. We knew that our rubber raft was a much superior craft for bouncing off rocks, for rubber is certainly more forgiving than wood. We also knew from maps a little about what actually lay ahead—something about which Powell could have only brooded. True, too, we had the comfort of knowing that others had made this run and done so satisfactorily. But at that moment it was impossible to be complacent, for we had thoroughly researched the challenges offered by the river. In fact, if anything, we had erred with too much research and were having difficulty establishing an appropriate mindset. We agonized about the sounds, struck with the knowledge that the only way back home was by passing through whatever waters the gods might unleash.

Powell had named the stretch of water we now heard for the events that had unfolded there. His "luck" at this precise area had come in twos and was akin to a one-two knock-down punch. The names said it all: Upper Disaster, followed swiftly by Lower Disaster. Their impact on Powell's expedition must have cast a gloom over the crew that was difficult to shrug off.

"I pass around a great crag," wrote Powell about Upper Disaster, "just in time to see the boat strike a rock . . . Two of the men lose their oars; she swings around and is carried down at a rapid rate, broadside on, for a few yards, when, striking amidships on another rock with great force, she is broken quite in two and the men are thrown into the river . . ."

Powell's experiences through this series of rapids weighed heavy on our minds, but his disaster was compounded by yet another condition. We knew that when Powell attempted his explorations, flows during his 9 June run approached 13,000 cfs. We also knew such high waters could elevate you above

# Green River Trip, Day 1

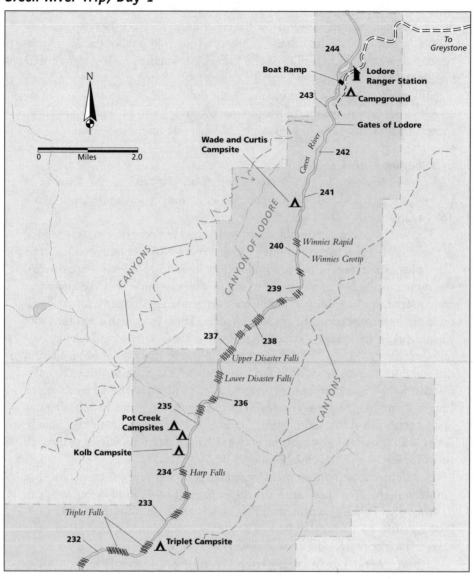

the level of the rocks, sometimes even smoothing your ride. Today, on the last weekend in May, waters on this same stretch were hammering the rocks at 6,000 cfs, and as we approached Upper Disaster, we were acutely aware of the tumult.

Upper Disaster spans about 0.25 mile, and we beached on the left bank of the river to scout the area. Not to do so would have been foolish. Then we climbed a steep hill that overlooked the Green. From our vantage the river actually looked worse than it sounded. Sure, we could portage. In fact, judging from the well-beaten path, many had. But wouldn't that diminish our experience?

As we mulled over that thought, we were greeted by the unexpected shouts of two men, both wearing ranger uniforms. "If you decide to make the run, stay to your right," said the oarsman. "Watch us."

With little ceremony the ranger entered the froth, then ferried behind a huge boulder that seethed and foamed with water. Behind the rock was an expansive hole, and some less turbulent waters were associated with that hole. Deftly the river ranger maneuvered behind the rock and ferried a short distance to river right. Then he repeated the maneuver—always relying on the less turbulent water—until he managed to avoid an awful roar of water on river left. By proceeding in a series of short ferries, he had positioned himself to the right of center, where waters were more user-friendly. Then he disappeared around a bend, allowing us to wallow in indecision.

Half an hour later we realized we could procrastinate no longer. We shoved our 14-foot boat into the river—and almost instantly were locked in the river's brawn.

I wish before we had left home that I had done more pushups or lifted more weights. Or that my last rafting experience had not been several years ago. What followed was a series of mistakes executed with precision that were a marvel to behold. In fact, you can use our performance as an example of what you should *not* do.

Immediately we broadsided the same rock the ranger had so easily shipped. Then, as I attempted to push off with the oar, the boat shot forward, knocking the oar from my hand and into the water. You should never allow that to happen.

Just before the oar shot past the boat's bow, Janie managed to reach out and snatch it from a watery fate. She thrust it toward me, and I desperately returned the oar pin to its lock. But during those few moments we had paid a price, for now the boat careened—utterly out of control.

Ultimately, the fates waxed kindly, but not without first presenting a series of challenges. Although I had committed two major blunders in rapid succession, I recovered and had the finesse to pull with my left arm and push with my right just as we slammed onto yet another rock, my actions whipping the raft from that rock and back into the current, which immediately thrust us onto yet another rock.

And now our raft had begun to fill with water.

Our boat is a bucket boat—one that you must bail yourself—and Janie attempted to do just that. But we were floating now through powerful waves, and our descent down this maelstrom was less than ideal. More water swallowed our boat until we were almost bathing in it. We were now in the midst of Upper Disaster, and we actually wallowed through—not with grace or dignity, but because *we had become one with the water!*

At the end of the rapids, we pulled over and began to bail. At first we attempted to muscle the raft onto its side. But water weighs eight pounds per cubic foot, and our 14- by 5-foot raft, filled with about 2.5 feet of water times eight, now totaled about 1,400 pounds. Still, it didn't take long until we could in fact heft the boat, dump the water, and launch. Physically we were ready to navigate Lower Disaster, and, after lashing our gear, we plunged back into the current.

We'd been told that the one benefit of floating Lower Disaster when water ran so high was that some of the rocks might be deeply submerged. Navigating, therefore, would be simplified. Our information was correct, but our source also explained that some of the other rapids that lay ahead had intensified and that we would want to examine each for potential danger. (That's something we did right, so here you'll want to follow our example.)

But our run was in the far distant future. It wasn't until tomorrow. Today we could either compartmentalize our fear or we could agonize.

We decided to agonize. You might, too, but we advise against it.

Several hours later we pulled into our campsite at the head of Triplet Falls. The campground was beautiful, but the howl of the rapids a hundred yards downstream created a resounding roar and muted our appreciation of the sheer brown- and rose-colored cliffs the river had cleaved. Later, from the glow of the setting sun, I read from Wallace Stegner's book about his interpretation of the roaring rapids. He confirmed that the rapids ahead could be exceedingly challenging. Ahead of us yet were Moonshine, School Boy, SOB, and Hell's Half Mile, and, of course, Triplet, the rapid creating the roar that would challenge us that night for sleep.

Next morning Janie informed me that she preferred to walk around the rapids. There is precedent for this strategy ("We make a portage around the first," wrote Powell, "past the second, and the third we let down with lines."), and I concurred with my wife, probably with some degree of alacrity.

Janie was particularly concerned about one rock in Triplet. Here the waters stream toward the boulder, creating on its downstream side a huge sinkhole.

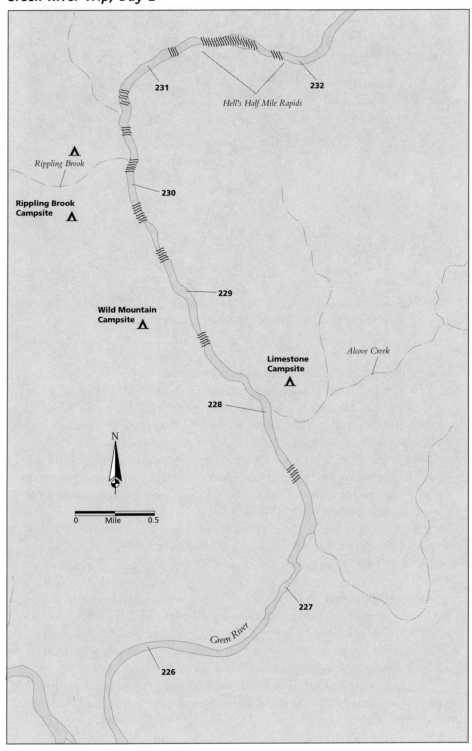

231

232

*Hell's Half Mile Rapids*

**⋀**
*Rippling Brook*

**Rippling Brook
Campsite** **⋀**

230

**Wild Mountain
Campsite** **⋀**

229

**Limestone
Campsite**
**⋀**

*Alcove Creek*

228

N

0  Mile  0.5

227

*Green River*

226

*Rafter Penny McDonald in Hell's Half Mile rapid on the Green River.*

Based on my performance yesterday, I understood her trepidation and deferred to her suggestion that she serve as the official photographer for Triplet.

Drifting into the rapids I followed the example of the ranger who had camped upstream and was passing us once again. He had eased broadside into the rapids, and I followed suit.

Initially the waves were relatively small, and in theory a broadside approach would enable one to power away from a series of nasty sinkholes toward which the insistent current rushed. A broadside approach would enable one to angle toward the cliff on river right, where the waves were not so horrendous. But to keep from slamming into the cliff wall, you then had to turn the raft 180 degrees and pull away from the rock face. Then you had to redirect the raft and power away from a huge rock before another nasty hole could swallow you whole.

Aware of the challenge, I worked hard not to repeat my mistakes of yesterday. To my great cheer, I did so satisfactorily. Perhaps I was beginning to regain some degree of competence. With great precision I executed my plan, picking up Janie just downstream of the rock that had so tormented us in our dreams.

Still, the worse was yet to come, for ahead lay Hell's Half Mile.

For Powell Hell's Half Mile had been a nightmare, and our imagination again began to play tricks. Again we could either compartmentalize our fear or we could agonize. This time we compartmentalized. After all, we were on one of America's most beautiful rivers, rich in history and Indian lore. At last we were beginning to realize that it would be foolish to remain in a perpetual state of apprehension, especially because (at Triplet) we were several hours yet from Hell's Half Mile.

What we had to do was to proceed with prudence. We also had to assume a more practical—perhaps an even more philosophical—approach. Surely we could handle Hell's Half Mile and all the rest. After all, many men and women before us had run these waters successfully. Throughout the river's entire history, only a few have perished. Statistically that meant Hell's Half Mile would pose less of a risk than talking on your cell phone while driving to Dinosaur. Though we had grappled with some fear and some misjudgment, we had, after all, gotten through some of the worst. We'd get through again—and you will, too, if you exercise prudence. If the rapids look bad, then portage. Otherwise, go for it. What it all comes down to is possessing the humility to assess one's capabilities.

## Ecstasy

Several hours after passing through Triplet, we drifted to Hell's Half Mile and immediately realized we needed to think this one over carefully. Here the waters gather together in one powerful surge and rush toward a huge rock that almost cost a rafting acquaintance his life. The rock is called Lucifer, and because of it Janie and I decided that perhaps this was one series of rapids around which we should portage. We both felt confident now that we could run the section, but caution prevailed. We were by ourselves, and, for that reason more than any other, we concluded that it would be wise to spend the several hours portaging.

We began by dismantling our cargo. Then we carried all our gear about 0.25 mile for a series of three complete round-trips. That put us well past Lucifer's Rock and a series of rocks that cut across the Green.

According to the handout provided by Dinosaur, Hell's Half Mile "probably can't be lined," though it can be portaged on the *right-hand* side with "lots of work." But for whatever reason—perhaps the water levels had altered things—we believed the raft could be lined fairly easily on river left. It looked far easier than a series we once lined in Alaska, and our assessment proved correct—with the exception of a short maze of rocks, where we simply lifted the raft on one side to prevent having to drag it. About an hour and a half later, we had reassembled and were ready to move on, no worse for the effort. Several hours later we reached Limestone, our designated campsite.

Next day we arose early, knowing we would be passing through one of the monument's most beautiful spots. We pushed off, and within the hour we began

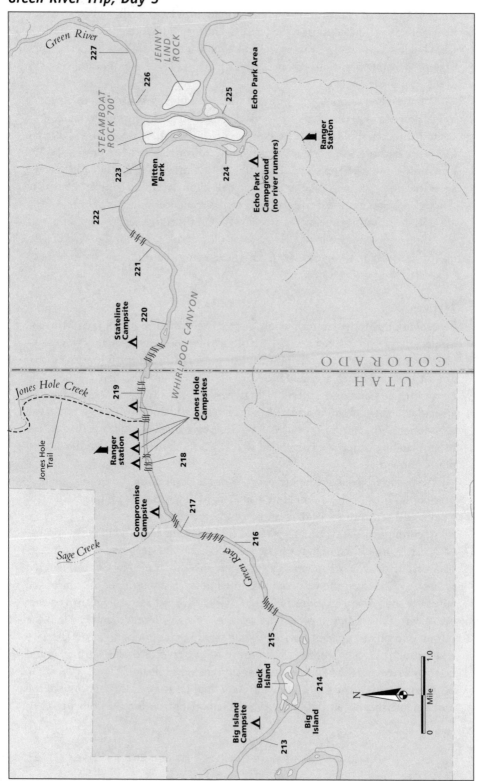

to encounter huge monolithic rocks, streaked with what a Navajo friend called Mother Nature's hair.

Actually the streaks represent millennia of work by bacteria that have chemically altered the manganese in the rock by "fixing" or combining with the available oxygen. The end result is the long lines of black streaking so common along Dinosaur's two rivers. Here, on the upstream side of Steamboat Rock, the streaking was particularly apparent. And so it remained for several miles as we passed the confluence of the Green with the Yampa at Echo Park.

So much can be said about Echo Park that we have reserved that discussion for a section of its own (see Chapter 6, Backcountry Driving Tours, page 36). Suffice it to say that Echo Park may be one of the world's most strikingly beautiful canyon areas. Unfortunately not all considered it worthy of preservation; back in the 1950s the Bureau of Reclamation had targeted this precise area for impoundment. About a mile downstream, the bureau wanted to place a dam that would have forever eliminated Echo Park, the Yampa, and the Green as they now exist in Dinosaur.

Late that afternoon we drifted into Jones Hole, our third night on the river. Here, according to our plan, we camped. Later that evening we hiked the 2 miles to Deluge Shelter on Jones Hole Trail to view some of the monument's pictographs. Again one of the motifs was sheep, but there were also strange symbols that could have been of the sun or some other cosmic element. On the way back we saw fresh sheep prints.

All along the way we had seen bighorn sheep. A ranger we'd encountered told us that the type we were seeing belonged to the Rocky Mountain bighorns, rather than the desert bighorn group. Because it was June, the ewes and lambs had separated from the rams. What's more, they appeared shaggy, which was perfectly normal; they were simply shedding their winter pelage. Next day a band of bighorns moved quietly along the far shore, and we felt privileged to see them.

The next day we departed Jones Hole with a group who had asked us to join them, riding together in a bargelike flotilla. As we drifted through the broad expanses of Island and Rainbow Parks, we were fortunate that the wind that had plagued us on our first day from Lodore had stilled.

As we drifted, our new friend Rob elevated an umbrella on his cataraft, and we gathered beneath its shade. We opened a cold drink and watched the herons and numerous families of geese. We saw more sheep, including one rather large ram, which though not quite a full curl was still large. From research I had conducted on bighorn sheep, I believed the ram to be about six years old.

Here in the shadow of land where dinosaurs once roamed, we watched an abundance of life as we drifted by. We talked of the huge quarry, where dinosaur bones littered an entire mountainside. We laughed at jokes and at one another's

*Green River Trip, Day 4*

N

0 — 1 Mile

To Vernal

Dirt Road

Ruple Ranch

214

Bobby Island

213

Ford Island

212

211

210

Island Park

Island Park Campground

209

Car-camp only

Rainbow Park

208

Boat ramp

207

*Green River*

206

Moonshine Rapid

SOB Rapid

205

Schoolboy Rapid

204

SPLIT MOUNTAIN

203

202

Inglesby Rapid

201

200

Split Mountain Campground

Boat Ramp Takeout

199

To Green River Campground

To 40

attempts to tell the best joke. The moment became one of those rare times of perfection, when nothing, absolutely nothing, seems out of place.

But the day of rapids was not over. About three hours later we left Rainbow Park and entered Split Mountain Canyon, where forces beneath the earth's surface had thrust mountains upward. Here lands that were once beneath inland seas and were formed from sediments of red, green, brown, and black now towered above as rocks of those same hues. Rain and snow, freezing and thawing, had broken them apart, sending them cascading into the river, where their presence now created much turbulence.

And now another series of rapids was upon us. But we were confident, and that manifested itself in better boatmanship. In a high state of exaltation, we passed through Moonshine Rapid, SOB, and then Schoolboy Rapid. Sure, we took on a bit of water, but very little, and the water we did take on was a result of large waves. When we descended into a trough, water from the crest of the next waiting wave tried to engulf us. Our little raft plowed through the waves well, in part because I had mastered a technique I had not used for some years, but which I quickly relearned. When approaching a wave that wants to flip you, keep your oars in the water. As you enter the wave, push forward to counteract the uplifting and backward thrusting effect of the wave. The technique worked for me and will for you.

As we passed around Split Mountain, we noted in the *Dinosaur River Guide* an entry Powell had made on 24 June 1869. "What a view!" he wrote. "The river cuts the mountain to its center, splitting the ridge for six miles, then turns out of it. All this we can see where we stand on the summit, and so we name the gorge below Split Mountain Canyon."

To that we can only concur. What a view, and how fortunate that we have preserved such rivers so that future generations can also learn to cope with fear, gather confidence, and exalt.

## Running the Rapids

For those who want to run the Green on their own, here are some suggestions amassed by Dinosaur's river rangers that pertain to specific rapids along the Green from Lodore to Echo Park. Generally, if you make it to this point, you've got the skills to go the rest of the way. What's more, although the rapids beyond Echo Park can be treacherous, by and large they consist mostly of heavy waves that can often be avoided—if that's what you want to do.

**Winnies/Little Stinker in Lodore Canyon.** Can be lined and/or portaged. At 6,600 cfs this rapid is not much different from a low-water run. Still rocks above the water. Lots of room on river right. Make a left run only if you have a little boat and want to play in the rapids. At 8,000 to 9,000 cfs, not much different, just bigger water. But a suck hole develops behind the rock. At 12,000 cfs, same but significant vertical change in water level from in front of to behind the rock.

**Upper Disaster in Lodore Canyon.** Effort to portage may be too great for degree of difficulty of rapid. Not much change in difficulty from a low-water run. The higher the flow, the easier to run the main channel. At 6,600 cfs it gets easier to make a left run. By 12,000 cfs the rock is underwater and it's a straight shot. The caution for this rapid is that the higher the water, the more the falls on the right-hand side develop.

**Lower Disaster in Lodore Canyon.** Scout this rapid even more carefully than usual. Pull over to river left and look at the holes at the bottom of this series. Walk downstream a little if you need to in order to see well enough to scout carefully. Can be lined and/or portaged. At this rapid the river wants to push the boater to the right wall, so people tend to run it left. The higher the water gets, the easier the left run is. But at the bottom end, where the channel starts to narrow, there's a rock that sits right of center. At 6,600 cfs at the center and left of center, there are some submerged rocks that make small standing waves. At 12,000 cfs there are two big submerged rocks that both fold toward the center and create a huge hole. Really skilled boaters can take the centerline and shoot the folds. Most boaters should take the very far left. This is the least forgiving section of the entire Lodore run at high water.

**Harp Falls in Lodore Canyon.** Effort to portage may be too great for degree of difficulty of rapid. At high water the waves just get bigger. At really high water the rapid creates some significant wave trains.

**Triplet in Lodore Canyon.** Effort to portage may be too great for degree of difficulty of rapid. At the upper end of this rapid, the rocks get covered at 6,600 cfs. As the water gets bigger, so do the holes. The right turn toward the wall flattens out. On the stretch along the wall, as the water gets higher there's more tendency to force the boater toward the wall. But there is more maneuvering room in the center. Run the bottom part of this rapid to the left. Higher waters create more maneuvering room on this part of the rapid.

Hell's Half Mile in Lodore Canyon. Probably can't be lined. Can be portaged on the right with lots of work. At 6,600 cfs it's the same run as usual; the water is just faster. The boater needs to be tighter in to the top rock to make the run behind the rock. The hole starts to flatten out. At 8,000 to 9,000 cfs, it's still the same run, but there is more latitude after the slot because the boater doesn't have so many rocks to deal with. Above 10,000 cfs it's the same run, but the boater can run right or left of the top rock. The tricky part at this water level is that the rows of rock that are perpendicular in low water make big standing waves that can flip a boat. Because of those waves, don't make the run too far right.

# The Yampa River

**GENERAL:** The Yampa River flows for 46 miles through Dinosaur National Monument. You can join a private raft company or float on your own with a permit.

**PERMITS:** Permits are required and awarded by lottery. Call the Dinosaur River Office at (970) 374–2468.

**FEATURES:** Last free-flowing river in the Colorado River Basin. Signature Cave, Mantle Cave, Cleopatras Couch, Echo Park, Indian Rock Art, Tiger Wall, and other towering cliffs offer a multitude of geological features. Once called Bear River by early-day trappers. Rapids of note include Tepee, Little Joe, Five Springs, Big Joe, and the infamous Warm Springs.

**ACCESS:** From Deerlodge Park in Colorado. Deerlodge Park lies 53 miles east of Dinosaur Monument Headquarters. From Jensen, Utah, take U.S. Highway 40 east for 25 miles to Colorado and the Monument Headquarters. Continue on US 40 for 37 more miles to a left

*Sand beach on the Yampa River.*

# Yampa River Overview

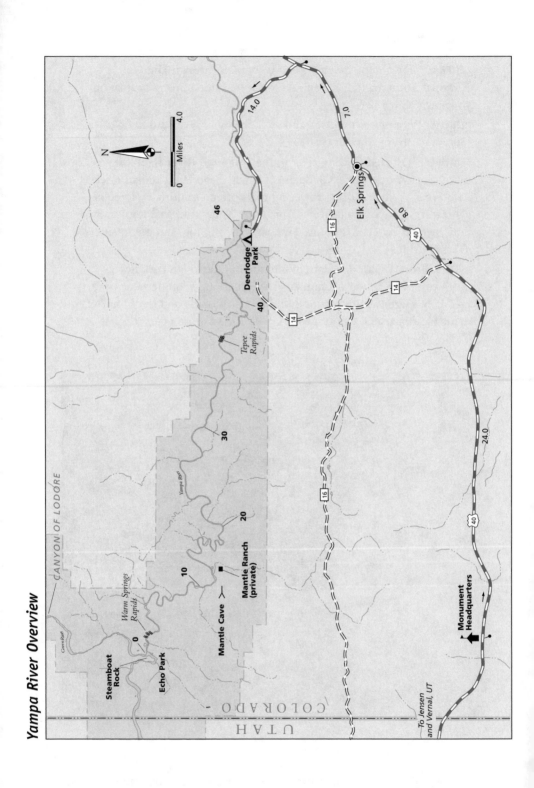

turnoff at the sign for Deerlodge Park. Go 17 miles on this well-paved road to Deerlodge Park and Campground and the Yampa River.

**TIME PERMITTED:** Trips down the Yampa usually entail four days; two days would be minimum with a takeout at Echo Park.

**CAMPSITES:** There are eight campsites on the Yampa River, which are assigned when your river permit is issued.

## Overview: The Yampa River

According to hydrologists, there is a rough law saying that the carrying power of water increases at the sixth power of its velocity. For example, a stream flowing at 2 miles an hour will carry particles sixty-four times as large as the same stream moving at 1 mile an hour. Applying the same principle, a stream moving 10 miles an hour will carry a rock a million times as great.

Consider now the power of the water that must have existed on 10 June 1965, when an immense flash flood carried rocks so huge that when the water slammed them against the canyon's walls, huge slabs were knocked loose from the cliff's face. When these slabs dropped they created a natural dam of house-sized boulders, as well as a series of rapids now called Warm Springs. Unfortunately the rapids that were formed caught a guide totally unprepared. That same week the unsuspecting guide entered this previously unchallenging section of the Yampa and was swept to his death. Because the waters here had always been so placid, the man was not wearing a flotation device.

Today everyone knows about Warm Springs Rapids, and most consider these rapids to be the monument's most difficult series to run. Essentially waters from these rapids power you around a canyon wall and then force you into a wave train that has limited maneuverability because of the juxtaposition of the canyon walls. Somehow, at the end of the train, you must avoid a major boulder that has flipped more than one good river runner. If you are not a well-qualified oarsman, here's one very good reason to join a guided group that includes a professional.

But whatever your capabilities, the Yampa is the one river everyone should learn to revere, for the Yampa is the last—the very last—of all the rivers in the immense Colorado River Basin that has eluded the grasp of those who believe all desert rivers are better when dammed. Put another way, no dams means a lot, for here the beautiful art left by Native Americans has not been covered with the silt of impoundment waters. Here most of the fish and wildlife that depend on wild canyons remain, and the river vegetation is in its natural state. Here, too, the towering multicolored canyons with all their beauty still have the power to awe mankind; they have not been reduced to tiny protrusions above a vast pool of water, such as found at Lake Powell or Flaming Gorge. For most these features help make the Yampa one of their favorite rivers.

*Duckies in Warm Springs Rapids on the Yampa River.*

Appropriately the Yampa has majestic beginnings, initiating its flow in the Flat Tops of northwestern Colorado outside the monument. Here the river gathers snowmelt and begins its journey to its confluence with the Green at Echo Park. Thus the river remains in Colorado for its entirety. Because the river's depth depends so much on runoff, the Yampa is best floated in spring and early summer. After early July the river generally dewaters to such an extent that the float becomes more of a drag—literally.

## Running the Yampa

For those who run the Yampa in Dinosaur, floats begin at Deerlodge Park, a broad valley in the far east corner of the monument where the Yampa spreads and moves along at relaxing pace. On the day of our guided float, the party consisted of five rafts. We floated along at a leisurely pace, giving us time to reflect with our guides on the origin of river rafting, much of which can be attributed to the Yampa and to the company (Hatch Expeditions) we had selected to transport us along this 46-mile-long corridor through Dinosaur.

One of the most noted techniques for running rivers began around the turn of the twentieth century by Nathaniel Galloway, a hunter and trapper who plied the Yampa. In his day it was the practice of river men to row with their backs to the danger. Galloway believed the loss of power was more than compensated for by turning around and facing the rapids. The move was simple yet radical, and even today oarsmen rowing in this fashion are said to be using the Galloway position. The position is now the preferred one used on all North American rivers by those using rubber rafts.

Galloway also began experimenting with different types of boats. According to river historian Roy Webb, one of the early boats contained watertight compartments created by using big carbide cans built into decks. "These," says Webb in his book *If We Had a Boat*, "had a screw-down lid with a gasket. Not only would they keep supplies and gear dry, they would provide extra flotation."

Many other changes have occurred since the days of Galloway. The raft used by our guide was a 16-foot self-bailer, and for the first 10 miles little was required of our guide other than to spin the boat for a better view. But several hours after we launched, we heard a dull roar signifying that things were about to change. Moments later, the roar grew louder, and then we were in the grips of the Yampa's first challenging series of rapids: Tepee Rapids.

Though Tepee Rapids has a reputation of brawn and power, on that late June day the water was down—about 3,000 cfs—and though exhilarating was not particularly challenging. This is another reminder as to just how much wild rivers can vary from day to day.

Indeed the Yampa is a wild river, as Jen Stark, our river guide, pointed out. Most significantly she noted the lack of the tamarisk trees, which were so numerous along the Green. Tamarisk trees are an exotic, introduced from the Mediterranean for ornamental purposes. Unfortunately the tree has flourished over much of the Southwest, outcompeting native species such as the cottonwood.

Stark also pointed out the abundance of cottonwood trees, so important in the region's ecology. Their presence was significant because of the bald eagle. Mature cottonwood trees provide the lofty branches free from predators that adult eagle pairs require for raising their young. The results are easily evaluated. Along the Yampa we saw eagles; along the Green we didn't.

In order for cottonwood trees to prosper, several things must happen. First, high waters must scour the riverbank free of debris and vegetation. Then spring waters must deposit a layer of silt. These conditions must continue for the next two or three years; otherwise, cottonwoods will be unable to establish themselves. On rivers that have consistent flows created by the regulation of impoundments, cottonwood trees cannot establish themselves, but other species can—such as the exotic water-guzzling tamarisks.

In addition to the more celebrated forms of wildlife, the Yampa also serves as a refuge for four species of endangered fish: the razorback sucker, the humpback chub, the Colorado pikeminnow, and the bonytail chub.

# Yampa River Trip, Day 1

Big Joe Campground

Big Joe Rapid

Five Springs Rapid

Little Joe Rapid

Yampa River

Tepee Campground

Tepee Rapids

Ponderosa Campground

Anderson Hole Campground

Deerlodge Park (el. 5,595')

Harding Hole Campsites

Night 1

N

Miles

0        3.0

Our first day of floating was an easy one. The mid-June day was warm, and it was easy to be lazy. The waters were moderate, and we scurried through Little Joe, Five Springs, and Big Joe Rapids before stopping for the night at Harding Hole. A long day—we had come 26 miles.

On the second day of our float, the tempo increased. For us it began by photographing six bighorn rams across the river. Shortly thereafter we loaded up. Quickly we approached Signature Cave. The cave is a substantial cavern that attracted a number of early-day river runners, such as Bus Hatch, to leave their names. But you should remember that they were historical figures—today's river runners should leave the walls without further adornment. Here is where Civil War veteran Pat Lynch sought out much-needed solitude. In a cave filled with Indian artifacts, Lynch wrote in less than perfect grammar:

> If in these caverns you shelter take
>   Please do them no harm
> Lave everything you find around
>   Hanging up or on the ground.

Just downstream is Mantle Cave, easily accessible from the river. Look first for the Mantle Ranch on river left at Mile 12. Here, several hundred yards downstream from the ranch, our guides pulled in for lunch. While they were setting up, a group of us followed a well-marked trail that threaded upward for about 0.25 mile to one of the river's most significant archaeological discoveries. Mantle Cave is a huge structure, perhaps the length of a football field. Several hundred years ago, when the Fremont Indians farmed the Yampa Valley, they would deposit their surplus corn in rock bins. On the day of our visit, though the banks along the river were hot, the cave was cool, a perfect refrigerator still protecting one last ear of corn, left (according to our guide) about A.D. 1200. Once the rock bins contained about 1,000 ears of corn, but through the years visitors have made off with the ears until only the one remains.

Archaeologists have also found many Indian artifacts in Mantle Cave, including a leather pouch containing a flicker feather headdress made of mule deer hide with the ears of the animal still attached. The dry elements in the cave also protected baskets made by these pre-Columbian Indians.

Back in the raft we floated on, some of us with a sense of premonition. Soon we would pass through Warm Springs Rapids, and we had all been briefed. Still we had little sense of turmoil. Above us towered gigantic cliffs laid down millions of years ago. We drifted on and soon encountered Tiger Wall, perhaps the monument's most magnificent specimen of streaked rock.

Tradition has it that as you pass the rock, to ensure a safe passage downstream, you must kiss the rock three times. Late in the season it is not difficult

## Yampa River Trip, Day 2

to fulfill the tradition. But guides warn that one rafter knocked loose three of his teeth early in the season. On this day the water was not particularly high. The lateness of the month had diminished the water's thrust, and Janie successfully ensured that our passage downstream would be a safe one—at least for her.

Not far ahead, we heard the roar of Warm Springs Rapids. Though lower water had diminished its violence, it was still a series that could maim unless treated with respect. Our guides (all five of them) insisted that they scout the rapids—despite the fact that several of them had run it recently. Stark told us this one should be run on the right.

Essentially two problems confront the rafter: One, you cannot allow the water's power to slam you into the cliff face on the left, which is the prevailing current's natural course. Two, after the cliff and the ensuing wave train, you must power away from the downstream boulder field.

We were the last raft to go through, since we took pictures of the others, including those who had the courage to run this rapid in "rubber duckies." Stark said she wanted to go in backward, but we didn't quite do that, so she swiftly reoriented us. Soon we were bouncing on an extended wave train and having a fine ride. Two miles later we arrived at Box Elder, our camp for the night. We'd traveled 18 miles that day.

Day three dawned cool but sunny. After another great camp breakfast, we loitered a bit. As river veterans now, we knew we could pack quickly. Besides, this would be a short mileage day—only about 8—ending at Jones Hole on the Green River.

Two miles more on the Yampa and we'd reached the confluence with the Green, heading straight for massive Steamboat Rock and Echo Park. At Echo Park we landed for a long break. Some of the group hiked up to Pat's Cave, Whispering Cave, Pool Creek Petroglyphs, and even on to the Chew Ranch. All of these excursions are destinations you should consider.

Next day we pulled out of Echo Park and glided through Mitten Park, a lovely open setting beneath the Mitten Park Fault. A mile later we reached Whirlpool Canyon and the site of the proposed (1955) Echo Park Dam. Thankfully this proposal was defeated, though a dam was constructed at Flaming Gorge.

Though waters in Whirlpool Canyon can at times be horrendous, on that day waters simply swirled in large and miniature whirlpools, which were not a major problem. In this canyon the calm water gave way to a series of unnamed riffles and small rapids. Five and a half miles from Echo Park, we struggled to pull in for the night at Jones Hole. It was overcast with a hint of rain, a harbinger of what tomorrow might offer. Hastily we unloaded our gear, set up tents, and then explored!

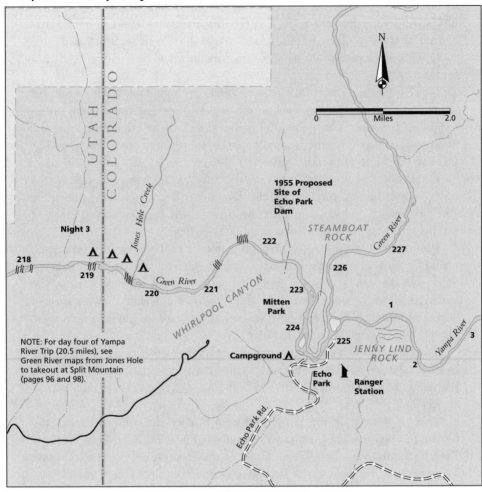

Beautiful Jones Creek flowed clear into the Green beside our camp, and some tried their luck at fly fishing. Others hiked up Jones Hole Trail about 2 miles to search for the petroglyphs at Deluge Shelter. Others just relaxed (remember, there's nothing wrong with simply kicking back and doing nothing) and watched our guides unwrap huge steaks and prepare a birthday cake for one of the rafters. As for us, we stayed up too late, knowing it was our last night on this incredible river and forgetting that we had 18.5 miles to go tomorrow, lots of it through big rapids.

Next morning it was raining and had turned colder. We left early, most of us bundled in our rain gear—equipment you'll regret not having should it rain and then blow (creating with the wind chill some frigid conditions, even in summer). At 3:00 P.M. we took out at Split Mountain, again feeling the letdown we had felt the previous week when we completed our float down the Green. The realization, of course, was that wild rivers had gotten into our blood, and that we'd miss them. But we'd be taking memories with us that would sustain us until we could strike forth again—which we knew we would.

# Appendix A
# Where to Stay While Visiting
# Dinosaur National Monument

If you are planning to camp while visiting Dinosaur National Monument, the area offers many options. Camping is a great idea, since many people find Dinosaur so interesting that they end up extending their stay. There are no motels or restaurants within the monument.

## Camping in the Monument

Ely Creek (the only designated backcountry campground) requires a permit; Split Mountain Campground (groups only in summer) and the Echo Park Campground group site require reservations during summer months. The other campgrounds are on a first-come, first-served basis. Recreational vehicles longer than 35 feet cannot be accommodated in any of the campgrounds, and there are no hookups in any campgrounds. There is a fourteen-day length-of-stay limit. According to current monument regulations, camping is permitted at accessible river camps on the Green and Yampa Rivers from the second Saturday in September to the second Sunday in May.

### Utah Campgrounds

**Split Mountain Campground** is 4 miles east of the dinosaur quarry. In summer it is open *for group camping only* and charges group fees with a maximum of twenty people at each of the four sites. Though there's no water in winter, the campground is open the rest of the year to individual campers. It offers water, restrooms, shade, tables, and firepits. For reservations call (435) 781–7759.

**Green River Campground** is 5 miles east of the dinosaur quarry with eighty-eight sites for tents and RVs. Many sites are shaded, and amenities include drinking water, restrooms, firepits, and picnic tables. Ranger talks are offered in the evenings. This campground is open from April until October with a $12 fee per night. Green River is closed during winter.

A nice path leaves from the north end of the campground. It winds above the Green River and in 1.8 miles ends at Split Mountain Campground. In early morning and late afternoon, great photo opportunities exist for both the river and Split Mountain. We saw lots of cacti along this moderately easy trail.

**Rainbow Park Campground** is located 26 miles from the dinosaur quarry. This is a primitive campground with two tent sites, no water, and pit toilets. It lies at the end of an unpaved road that is impassable when wet. *No RVs are*

*Setting up camp at Echo Park Campground.*

*allowed.* The campground is open year-round (weather permitting), and there is no fee.

**Ely Creek Campground** is the monument's only designated backcountry campground. Located 2 miles down Jones Hole Creek Trail, it offers two large primitive tent sites along Jones Creek with enough room for ten people at each site. No water, no fires, no mountain bikes, no pets, no fees. Camping by free backcountry permit only, available at the dinosaur quarry or Headquarters Visitor Center. A Utah fishing license is required to fish the creek.

## Colorado Campgrounds

**Echo Park Campground** is 38 miles north of Dinosaur Monument Headquarters, off Harpers Corner Road. The last 13 miles of road are unpaved and extremely rough; no trailers or RVs. The road becomes impassable when wet. There are seventeen tent sites, five walk-in sites, and one group site. Drinking water is available, and each site has a table. No fires allowed. The fee is $8.00 per night. There are weekend ranger talks and walks, so sometimes this popular place fills on the weekends. Echo Park is closed in winter by snow.

**Deerlodge Park Campground** is 53 miles east of Dinosaur Monument Headquarters. This eight-site campground has no water and no camping fees and is open year-round. It does offer shade, pit toilets, tables, and fireplaces. This campground is often used as the put-in point for those floating the Yampa River, but after mid-July it is nearly deserted. This quiet, peaceful place offers fishing in the Yampa, hiking around the area, or just plain relaxing. Open in winter, depending on road conditions.

**Gates of Lodore Campground** is in the remote Browns Park area, 120 miles north of Dinosaur Monument Headquarters. Little used, it's in a lovely setting right on the Green River at the entrance to Lodore Canyon and offers a base while you explore Browns Park. River runners camp here, as this is the put-in point for multiday trips on the Green River. It is open all year for tents and RVs and has shade, water, pit toilets, tables, and fire pits. The fee is $8.00 per night. A ranger is stationed at the campground. This campground is open in winter, depending on road conditions, though there is no water (and no fee) then.

## Backcountry Camping in the Monument

As there is no large designated trail system in Dinosaur, backcountry hiking is an option for some. With a good U.S. Geological Survey or National Geographic Trails Illustrated topo map, you can spend many days in the backcountry. You'll need a free backcountry permit from a ranger or from one of the visitor centers in order to camp in the wilderness. Rangers and visitor centers can make good suggestions as to the best campsites. For information phone (970) 374–3000.

## Camping Outside the Monument

There are commercial campgrounds and RV parks located near the monument in Vernal (20 miles west of Douglass Dinosaur Quarry) and in Jensen (7 miles south of the quarry), both in Utah. In Colorado the towns of Dinosaur, Rangely, Craig, and Massadona have campgrounds.

The larger town of Vernal offers a good selection of motels. Others may be found in Dinosaur, Rangely, and Craig.

For further information contact the appropriate chamber of commerce:

    Vernal Area     (435) 789–1352
    Craig Area      (970) 824–5689
    Rangely Area    (970) 675–5290

**Addresses:**       Dinosaur National Monument
4545 East U.S. Highway 40
Dinosaur, CO 81610-9724
(970) 374–3000

Intermountain Natural History Association
1291 East U.S. Highway 40
Vernal, UT 84078-2830
(435) 789–8807

**Headquarters Visitor Center,** located 2 miles east of Dinosaur, Colorado, on US 40 is open daily from 8:00 A.M. to 4:30 P.M., Memorial Day through Labor Day. It is closed on weekends and holidays from October to Memorial Day.

**Dinosaur Quarry Visitor Center,** located 7 miles north of Jensen, Utah, on Utah Highway 149 is open 8:00 A.M. to 4:30 P.M. daily except Thanksgiving, Christmas, and New Year's Days. From Memorial Day to Labor Day, the Quarry Center is open 8:00 A.M. to 7:00 P.M.

**Dinosaur National Monument Web address:** www.nps.gov/dino/. This excellent Web site is filled with information, from a thorough overview of the monument to tips for planning a trip with children. The first page has all the hyperlinks you'll need.

**Camping:** To reserve a group campsite at Split Mountain Campground or the Echo Park group site in spring and summer, call (435) 789–8277. For back-country camping permits, call (970) 374–3000.

**River permits:** To apply for noncommercial river permits and information on fees, equipment, and related paperwork, call (970) 374–2468.

**Other activities requiring permits:**
Backcountry camping and horse packing: (970) 374–3000
Research collecting: (970) 374–3000

Special events: (970) 374–3000
Commercial photography or filming: (435) 781–7702
Commercial activity: (970) 374–3019

**Maps:** National Geographic Trails Illustrated Maps. For map purchase and information, write Intermountain Natural History Association, 1291 East U.S. Highway 40, Vernal, UT 84078-2830; e-mail topomaps@aol.com; or visit www.colorado.com/trails. Most maps can be purchased at the bookstores at Douglass Dinosaur Quarry or Headquarters Visitor Center. A fine selection is offered, as well as many excellent brochures produced by the Intermountain Natural History Association.

A number of companies offer commercial trips down the Green and Yampa Rivers. Because waters entering the Green are controlled at Flaming Gorge Reservoir, the high-water season and thus the season of usage is longer on the Green than on the Yampa.

## Raft Companies

The following companies offer multiday trips:

Adrift Adventures (trips from one or more days)
P.O. Box 903
Half Moon Bay, CA 94019
(435) 789–3600 (summer only)
(800) 824–0150

Adventure Bound
2392 H Road
Grand Junction, CO 81505
(800) 423–4668
Fax: (303) 241–5633

American River Touring Association
24000 Casa Loma Road
Groveland, CA 95321
(209) 962–7873
(800) 323–2782

Dinosaur River Expeditions
P.O. Box 3387
Park City, UT 84060
(435) 649–8092
(800) 345–RAFT

Eagle Outdoor Sports
1507 South Haight Creek Drive
Kaysville, UT 84037
(801) 451–7238

Hatch River Expeditions (trips of one or more days)
P.O. Box 1150
Vernal, UT 84078
(435) 789–4316
(800) 342–8243
www.hatchriver.com

Holiday Expeditions
544 East 3900 South
Salt Lake City, UT 84107
(801) 266–2087
(800) 624–6323

National Outdoor Leadership School (NOLS)
288 Main Street
Lander, WY 82520
(307) 332–6973
(435) 781–0305

Outdoor Adventure River Specialists (OARS)
P.O. Box 67
Angels Camp, CA 95222
(209) 736–4677
(800) 346–6277

## Shuttle Services

Wilkins Bus Lines: (435) 789–2476
River Runners Transport: (435) 781–1120

## Weather: What to Expect

As in many other states, March and April are often mud season, when the snow is finally melting. May can be very nice—even warm—but there is still the chance of snow, and nights are often quite cool. June, July, and August bring warmer, often hot daytime temperatures, but it is cooler in the canyons and higher elevations. Afternoon thunderstorms are common. According to the park, September and October bring the best weather. Winter brings snow and fog. Days are cold, and nights can be -20 degrees Fahrenheit. Don't forget: This is high-desert country, with elevations from 4,500 to 9,000 feet.

## What to Bring

Sturdy hiking boots, sneakers
Sunglasses
Binoculars
A broad-brimmed hat for sun
Sunscreen
Insect repellant
Shorts, long pants
Rain gear
A lightweight jacket and a heavy jacket
Clothing that can be layered
A five-gallon freshwater container to carry in your vehicle. (Often you stop or end up camping in a place where no fresh water is available.) Or carry a good water filtration system to use in rivers or creeks.

Pets are not allowed on trails, in boats, in the backcountry, or in visitor centers. Where they're allowed, dogs must be on a leash at all times. This leads to a very unhappy pet if you intend to go off exploring for any length of time. Pets should never be locked in a car and left unattended.

## General River Trip Tips

The Dinosaur River Office is quite explicit on items you must have before you may launch your own watercraft. When you apply for a permit, you will be sent a complete list. Everyone is checked in by a ranger before starting off on the rivers. Some of the required items include a metal strainer, approved life jackets, a first-aid kit, a throw (rescue) rope, a fire pan, a groover for multiday trips, an extra paddle, and a bailer.

If you are planning to run the rivers on your own, you probably already know exactly what personal items to bring, but we suggest the following as really nice additions:

A good water purifier system
Flashlight or headlamp
A wet suit
Cold-weather gear
Water sandals
Sunscreen and lots of good hand lotion
A small dunk bag to hold items that can get wet (like your water bottle and sunscreen)
Extra carabiners
Baby wipes
Rowing gloves

If you are going on a river trip with a professional guide outfit, they'll let you know what to bring. Mostly it's just your clothing (for hot and cold and rainy days), your camera, and personal items. You can bring your own tent and sleeping bag for multiday trips, or you can rent them from the outfit. If you like to munch on special snacks in your tent at night, you'll have to bring those, too!

*All Things Checklist*, produced and funded by the Intermountain West Natural History Association, Vernal, Utah.

*Beyond the Hundredth Meridian (John Wesley Powell and Second Opening of the West)* by Wallace Stegner. Penguin Books USA Inc., New York, 1953.

*Bighorn Sheep: Mountain Monarchs* by Bert Gildart. Creative Publishing, Northword Press, Minnetonka, Minnesota, 1999.

*Canyon Country Prehistoric Rock Art* by F. A. Barnes. Wasatch Publishers, Salt Lake City, Utah, 1982.

*Complete Whitewater Rafter, The*, by Jeff Bennett. Ragged Mountain Press, Camden, Maine, 1996.

*Dinosaur's Restless Rivers and Craggy Canyon Walls* by W. R. Hansen. Intermountain West Natural History Association, Vernal, Utah, 1996.

*Dinosaur River Guide* by Buzz Belknap and Loie Belknap Evans. Westwater Books, Evergreen, Colorado, fourth printing, revised edition, 2000.

*Echo Park Struggle for Preservation* by Jon M. Cosco. Johnson Printing, Boulder, Colorado, 1995.

*Exploration of the Colorado River and Its Canyons, The*, by J. W. Powell. Dover Publications, New York, 1961.

*Exploring the Fremont* by David B. Madsen. Utah Museum of Natural History, 1989.

*Geologic Map of Dinosaur National Monument and Vicinity, Utah and Colorado*, by Wallace R. Hansen, Peter D. Rowley, and Paul E. Carrara. Published by the U.S. Geological Survey, Denver, Colorado, 1983.

*If We Had a Boat* by Roy Webb. University of Utah Press, Salt Lake City, Utah, 1986.

*Plant List*, compiled by a park botanist, printed by Intermountain West Natural History Association, Vernal, Utah, 1996.

*River: One Man's Journey down the Colorado* by Colin Fletcher. Vintage Books, New York, 1998.

*Riverman, The Story of Bus Hatch*, by Roy Webb. Labyrinth Publishing, Rock Springs, Wyoming, 1989.

*Vernal Area Rock Art* by Byron Loosle, Ph.D., and Kelda Wilson, M.A. Copyright Byron Loosle, 1998.

*Whitewater Rafting* by William McGinnis. Times Books, The New York Times Book Co., Inc., New York, 1975.

*Wild Country Companion* by Will Harmon. Falcon, Guilford, Connecticut, 1994.

Cabela's: www.cabelas.com (800–237–4444)
Campmor: www.campmor.com (800–226–7667)
Cascade Outfitters: www.cascadeoutfitters.com
Dinosaur National Monument: www.nps.gov/dino
Dinosaur's rivers: www.nps.gov/dino/river
Topo maps: topomaps@aol.com

Bert and Janie Gildart share an enthusiasm for adventure, hiking, photography, natural history, and wilderness areas.

Bert is a member of the Outdoor Writers Association of America and the Northwest Outdoor Writers Association. He is the author of more than 300 magazine articles and nine books. He's been exploring and writing about the outdoors for the past twenty-five years and has served as a backcountry ranger in Glacier National Park.

Janie is a member of the Northwest Outdoor Writers Association. Together, she and Bert have written several books for The Globe Pequot Press, including *Hiking South Dakota's Black Hills Country, Hiking Shenandoah National Park, Best Easy Day Hikes Shenandoah National Park,* and *A FalconGuide to Death Valley National Park.*

The Gildarts make their home in northwest Montana.

# THE INSIDER'S SOURCE

With more than 540 West-related titles, we have the area covered. Whether you're looking for the path less traveled, a favorite place to eat, family-friendly fun, a breathtaking hike, or enchanting local attractions, our pages are filled with ideas to get you from one state to the next.

For a complete listing of all our titles, please visit our Web site at www.GlobePequot.com. The Globe Pequot Press is the largest publisher of local travel books in the United States and is a leading source for outdoor recreation guides.

# FOR BOOKS TO THE WEST